T0323772

Cambridge Elements ☰

Elements in The Aegean Bronze Age
edited by
Carl Knappett
University of Toronto
Irene Nikolakopoulou
Hellenic Ministry of Culture, Archaeological Museum of Heraklion

AEGEOMANIA

Modern Reimaginings of the Aegean Bronze Age

Nicoletta Momigliano
University of Bristol

CAMBRIDGE
UNIVERSITY PRESS

Shaftesbury Road, Cambridge CB2 8EA, United Kingdom

One Liberty Plaza, 20th Floor, New York, NY 10006, USA

477 Williamstown Road, Port Melbourne, VIC 3207, Australia

314–321, 3rd Floor, Plot 3, Splendor Forum, Jasola District Centre,
New Delhi – 110025, India

103 Penang Road, #05–06/07, Visioncrest Commercial, Singapore 238467

Cambridge University Press is part of Cambridge University Press & Assessment,
a department of the University of Cambridge.

We share the University's mission to contribute to society through the pursuit of
education, learning and research at the highest international levels of excellence.

www.cambridge.org
Information on this title: www.cambridge.org/9781009538930

DOI: 10.1017/9781009319089

First published 2024

A catalogue record for this publication is available from the British Library.

ISBN 978-1-009-53893-0 Hardback
ISBN 978-1-009-31909-6 Paperback
ISSN 2754-2998 (online)
ISSN 2754-298X (print)

Aegeomania

Modern Reimaginings of the Aegean Bronze Age

Elements in The Aegean Bronze Age

DOI: 10.1017/9781009319089
First published online: October 2024

Nicoletta Momigliano
University of Bristol
Author for correspondence: Nicoletta Momigliano, n.momigliano@bristol.ac.uk

Abstract: This Element provides an overview of Aegeomania: the fascination, sometimes bordering on the obsession, with the Aegean Bronze Age, which manifests itself in the uses of Aegean Bronze Age material culture to create something new in literature, the visual and performing arts, and many other cultural practices. It discusses the role that Aegeomania can play in our understanding of the Aegean Bronze Age and illustrates this with examples from the 1870s to the present, which include, among many others, poems by Emma Lazarus, Salvatore Quasimodo, and Giorgos Seferis; novels by Kristmann Gudmundsson, Mary Renault, Don DeLillo, Zeruya Shalev, and Sally Rooney; Freudian psychoanalysis; sculptures by Henry Moore and Pablo Picasso; music by Harrison Birtwistle and the rock band Giant Squid; films by Robert Wise and Wolfang Petersen; elegant textiles and garments created by Josef Frank and Karl Lagerfeld. This title is also available as Open Access on Cambridge Core.

Keywords: reception of Aegean archaeology, reception of Minoan archaeology, reception of Mycenaean archaeology, reception of Cycladic archaeology, reception of Trojan archaeology

ISBNs: 9781009538930 (HB), 9781009319096 (PB), 9781009319089 (OC)
ISSNs: 2754-2998 (online), 2754-298X (print)

Contents

1 Introduction: Aegeomania and the Archaeology of the Aegean Bronze Age

Kunst gibt nicht das Sichtbare wieder, sondern macht sichtbar
(Art does not reproduce what is visible, but makes visible)
Klee, Tribüne der Kunst und Zeit: Eine Schriftensammlung XIII. Schöpferische Konfession

In *Archaeology, Nation, and Race: Confronting the Past, Decolonizing the Future in Greece and Israel*, Yannis Hamilakis remarked that 'indigenous archaeologies' (which other scholars have called 'archaeophilia' and 'vernacular antiquarianism'), are often considered to have literary and folkloristic value, but no serious historical and/or archaeological importance, despite the fact that they offer a distinctive epistemic perspective and 'a rich body of ideas, discourses (often tacit), and practices that can fertilize our understanding and perception of antiquities' (Greenberg & Hamilakis, 2022: 88–90). To a large extent, the same applies to the phenomenon of Aegeomania, which some people still perceive as marginal (if not irrelevant) to conventional, proper archaeological research, despite the existence of a significant and growing body of work on the relationship between modern art, literature, and archaeology (e.g. Renfrew, 2003; Renfrew *et al.*, 2004; Wallace, 2004; Russell & Cochrane, 2015a, 2015b; Bailey, 2015, 2017; Piperno *et al.*, in the press; and the recent 'The Many Lives of a Snake Goddess' project: https://mlsg.squarespace.com). Aegeomania, like 'indigenous archaeologies', can equally enrich our appreciation and interpretation of the Aegean Bronze Age, as I hope to illustrate in the following pages.

But, first, what do I mean by Aegeomania? In this context, I use Aegeomania as a convenient term (modelled on the older Egyptomania, Graecomania, Hellenomania, and Cretomania) that indicates a fascination, sometimes bordering on an obsession, for things pertaining to the Aegean Bronze Age.[1] This fascination (or obsession) manifests itself in the uses, allusions, and citations of Aegean Bronze Age material culture in a wide variety of modern cultural practices, from literature to the visual and performing arts, and from architecture to fashion, neo-pagan

---

[1] Since the 1890s (cf. Petrie, 1890), the term Aegean has usually been associated with the Bronze Age period in Greece (3rd and 2nd millennia BC) in archaeological contexts. I have used the term Aegeomania (in the sense of the dynamics between modern cultural practices and Aegean Bronze Age material culture) in lectures I gave in 2016 at various university venues (e.g. Bristol, Nottingham, Reading) and in a very short essay (4,500 words including bibliography) titled 'Aegeomania: Aegean Influences on Contemporary Art', accepted by the editors of *A Companion to Aegean Art and Architecture* (Oxford: Blackwell) in 2016, but still unpublished at the time of my writing this Element (2023–4). The term Aegeomania has also been used in 2018 in the title of a modern art exhibition at the Alegria Estates (Mykonos, Greece), but in this case it referred to a fascination with the Aegean in broader conceptual and geographical terms (see https://tsiaras.com/aegeomania-exhibition-at-alegria-estates-mykonos-greece/).

religion, and even psychoanalysis, among many others (for the earlier terms Cretomania, Egyptomania, and Hellenomania see Momigliano, 2017a: 1–3; Harloe & Momigliano, 2018: 8–9; Momigliano, 2020: 2–3, with further references). In other words, Aegeomania indicates the borrowing and reimagining of elements pertaining to the archaeology of the Aegean Bronze Age to create something new, as attested since the 19th century.

This definition of Aegeomania is directly relevant to the archaeology of the Aegean Bronze Age and justifies what, at first sight, may appear as strange omissions, such as Minotaur images in famous paintings by Pablo Picasso and other artists. These works are omitted because they show no clear engagement with the material culture, iconography, and styles of the Aegean Bronze Age and, arguably, owe much more to Ovid's *Metamorphoses* and other classical sources (see Momigliano, 2020: 12). Similarly, I do not deal with representations of Troy, Mycenae, the Knossian labyrinth, and similar themes, which were produced well before the rediscovery of the Aegean Bronze Age made by archaeologists in the 19th and 20th centuries and were not inspired or influenced by the material culture of the Aegean Bronze Age, but by Graeco–Roman texts and artefacts. In fact, and perhaps rather surprisingly, even some modern works inspired by Heinrich Schliemann show only a limited engagement with the actual archaeology of the sites that he excavated. Examples of this are Betsy Jolas' 1995 opera *Schliemann* (premiered in Lyon in 1995) and its 2016 remake, titled *Iliade l'amour*, both inspired by Bruno Bayen's play, *Schliemann, Épisodes Ignorés* (Bayen, 1982; see also Jolas & Menesse, 2013), which show limited interest in the material culture of Troy, Mycenae, and other sites explored by the German businessman-cum-archaeologist. Even Peter Ackroyd's intriguing novel, *The Fall of Troy* (2006), which conflates the characters of Schliemann and Sir Arthur Evans, shows more engagement with the finds made by the latter (and by other archaeologists) at Knossos than with Schliemann's own discoveries in the Troad.[2] It is as if Schliemann's remarkable rags-to-riches story, his mendacity, and his relationship with his second wife (Sophia Engastromenou) have overshadowed his archaeological finds. Indeed, when it comes to modern reimaginings of Troy and the Trojans, it is curious to see that in many Aegeomanic works they are often provided with material culture inspired by Minoan Crete rather than their own.

---

[2] Ackroyd's novel presents sparse descriptions of Trojan objects, which are often rather fanciful, such as the mention of 'a spoon of silver, with a large omphalos' (Ackroyd, 2006: 42), which is difficult to match with any of Schliemann's finds, while those pertaining to Knossos are more accurate, take up more pages, and include mentions of clay tablets inscribed with linear signs and of children's bones with butchery marks (Ackroyd, 2006: 118, 119, 143, 144, 168), which are clear references to the Linear A and Linear B tablets from Knossos and to the gruesome discovery made by Peter Warren in the summer of 1979 (cf. Section 6.1).

But how can Aegeomania contribute to a better understanding of the Aegean Bronze Age? Or, to put it in other words, why should Aegean Bronze Age specialists (and specialists working in germane fields) pay any attention to this phenomenon? I believe that they should do so for several reasons.

First, if one defines archaeology as 'the discourses and practices involving material things of a past time' (Hamilakis, 2011: 52), Aegeomanic works could obviously be regarded as a form of Aegean Bronze Age archaeology. But even if one rejects this definition of archaeology as too broad to be useful in practice, and resorts to a more traditional characterization (e.g. archaeology as the study of the human past through material remains), Aegeomania still matters, since it contributes to the history of Aegean Bronze Age archaeology at least in terms of the intellectual and material consequences that this phenomenon has exerted on the development of this archaeological subdiscipline. This is because Aegeomania (like Egyptomania and other similar 'manias') entails two processes: on the one hand, archaeological finds and methodologies have inspired artists, writers, psychoanalysts, and other practitioners who are not professional archaeologists; on the other, these practitioners have affected the response to archaeological finds and interpretations.

For example, a lingering of classicizing aesthetics in the 1870s, and the initial controversy over the actual date and character of Schliemann's discoveries at Mycenae, partly explain the lukewarm reception of his discoveries in some quarters: to many people, his finds did not look Greek enough and some scholars, at the time, believed them to be Phoenician, Scythian, or even Byzantine; it was only the work of Tsountas in Greece and Petrie in Egypt during the 1890s that securely dated them to the late 2nd millennium BC and led to the enthusiastic connection between Aegean Bronze Age material culture and Greek mythical, heroic past (Fitton, 1995: 182; McDonald & Thomas 1990: 15, 71; for an immediate wholehearted reception, however, see the poem by Emma Lazarus discussed in Section 2.2). By contrast, the emergence and establishment of modernist artistic movements, such as Art Nouveau, paved the way for the immediate enthusiastic reception of Minoan Crete a generation later, since aspects of Minoan iconography (e.g. focus on essential lines, movement, and colour) chimed with modernist trends at the time and made Minoan Crete look modern and familiar (Momigliano, 2017b: 89; 2020: 38–41, 74–5, 86). These different receptions, in turn, contributed to interpretations of Minoan culture as original and full of *joie de vivre*, and of Mycenaean culture as derivative and dull – interpretations that were common in the early 20th century and persisted in subsequent decades.

Moreover, one may suggest that forms of Aegeomania have influenced Aegean Bronze Age scholars in their own specialist writings and in their career choices. For example, Emily Vermeule wrote in a well-known handbook of Aegean prehistory that Minoan Crete appeared in some works as 'a refined and pastel brothel where the sturdy [Mycenaean] mainlanders found experience and sophistication which they put to more manly uses after destroying the corrupters of their adolescence' (Vermeule, 1964: ix) – a comment that seems inspired by some Aegeomanic novels and by fanciful artistic illustrations used in some specialist works (e.g. Bossert, 1921, with illustrations by F. Krischen; see also Momigliano, 2020: 96, fig. 4.1a, b). Regarding Aegeomanic novels, an anecdote dating to the early 1980s reports that the Regius Professor of Greek at Oxford recommended reading Mary Renault's works for an insight into the Greek past (Sweetman, 1993: 303; see also Section 5.2). In fact, Renault's novels inspired the interest in the Aegean Bronze Age of a doyen of this discipline, Oliver Dickinson, who read them as an adolescent (Momigliano, 2020: 240), while another leading Aegean scholar, Jan Driessen, to use his own words, 'became hooked on Minoan Crete after reading *De Ramkoning* by Rose Gronon … [a book published in 1962 that] is all about Klytaimnestra, Crete, and female power'.[3]

Another example of why Aegeomania matters for the history of Aegean archaeology can be found in the consequences created by the growing status (and Aegeomania) of artists such Constantin Brâncuşi, Jacob Epstein, Alberto Giacometti, Barbara Hepworth, Amedeo Modigliani, Henry Moore, and Pablo Picasso in the interwar period, some of whom owned Aegean Bronze Age figurines from the Cyclades, and/or were influenced by them in their own works (Fitton, 1989; Renfrew, 1991; Gill & Chippindale, 1993; Renfrew, 2003: 50–8; Chryssovitsanou, 2004; Bach, 2006; Chryssovitsanou, 2006; see also Section 4.6). In the 18th and 19th centuries AD, Cycladic figurines were considered rather unattractive curiosities, but by the mid 20th century they had become highly desirable *objets d'art*, thanks to the fashion for primitivism and their perceived affinity with the modernist paintings and sculptures of artists like those mentioned earlier. Since then, these Cycladic objects have been sought after by collectors, who nowadays would willingly pay seven- and even eight-figure sums to buy them.[4] The attempt to satisfy the demands of the antiquity market resulted in the looting and destruction of many Bronze Age sites in the Cyclades, especially in the 1960s, and other illegal activities (see also Section 5.4).

---

[3] Personal communication (email of 4 January 2024, quoted by kind permission of Jan Driessen).

[4] Gill and Chippindale (1993: 607) report a seven-figure sum, while it has been recorded that on 9 December 2010 a Cycladic figurine was sold for US$16,882,500 at Christie's in New York (see www.christies.com/features/cycladic-art-a-guide-for-new-collectors-9983-1.aspx, and www.chris ties.com/lot/lot-a-cycladic-marble-reclining-female-figure-name-piece-5385394/.

Second, by contributing to a better understanding of the history of Aegean Bronze Age archaeology, Aegeomania may also help towards its decolonization, since this requires an appreciation of how a discipline was first 'colonized', via an understanding of its developments from the 19th century to the present. Thus, for example, the study of the intersections between Aegean Bronze Age archaeology and other disciplines, from literature to psychoanalysis, may help to illustrate how this past has been constructed and reimagined at times through racist, Eurocentric, colonial, and gender-obsessed terms.

Third, Aegeomania can contribute to an understanding of the Aegean Bronze Age because modern reimaginings of the material culture and people of this period can be 'good to think with.'[5] Modern uses of, and responses to, the Aegean Bronze Age in the works of non-specialists (and specialists alike) are subjective and historically contingent, but they all relate to specific Aegean Bronze Age features – whether it is the imposing Mycenaean and Trojan fortifications or the exposed breasts in Minoan female imagery – and they can stimulate different ways of thinking about the material culture of the Aegean Bronze Age. Although Aegeomanic works often appear merely to reaffirm dominant scholarly narratives and orthodoxies, at other times they modify or even question them, in ways that intersect with and sometimes anticipate debates among specialists. For example, as observed by Roderick Beaton (2006: 185), Nikos Kazantzakis' description of the final fall of Knossos in his epic poem *The Odyssey: A Modern Sequel* (1938; English translation 1958), with its stress on the insurgence of palace slaves, is reminiscent of the Bolshevik storming of the Winter Palace. But one could add that, by stressing social inequality, Kazantzakis foreshadowed later interpretations of the fall of the Aegean palaces in Marxist or almost-Marxist terms (cf. Andronikos, 1954; Chadwick, 1976; Halstead, 1988; Jung, 2016). Similarly, Dmitri Merezhkovsky's 1925 novel *The Birth of the Gods* characterized Minoan art as being made 'to destroy the eternal, to perpetuate the momentary, to arrest the flying', and anticipates Henrietta Groenewegen-Frankfort's well-known description of Minoan art in her *Arrest and Movement* (1951) as absolute mobility and disregard for timelessness.[6] Incidentally, Merezhkovsky's novel also anticipates the curious (and unproven) suggestion that Minoan Crete had an order of transvestite priests,

---

[5] Compare the famous sentence by the French anthropologist Claude Levi Strauss 'Les espèces sont choisies non commes bonnes à manger, mais comme bonnes à penser', often translated as 'good to think with' (see e.g. Culler, 2013). Eloquent discussions of the use of modern art in archaeological interpretation can be found in some works already mentioned (such as Renfrew, 2003).

[6] Merezhkovsky (1926 [1925]): 40. This can be compared with the following sentence by Groenewegen-Frankfort: 'Here and here alone [Minoan Crete] the human bid for timelessness was disregarded in the most complete acceptance of the grace of life the world has ever known. For life means movement and the beauty of movement; was woven in the intricate web of living forms which we call "scenes of nature", was revealed in human bodies acting their serious games

who 'were probably eunuchs', which appears in a popular and popularizing volume on the Minoans (Castleden, 1990: 140).

Perhaps more interesting, in the context of why Aegeomanic works can be 'good to think with', is Marc Chagall's 1925 drawing *L'écuyère*, which could be read as an irreverent take on the famous 'Toreador fresco' from Knossos. In Chagall's work all genders are altered: the Minoan bull becomes a gelding or a mare, the bull-leaper a woman, and the attendants are male. This, albeit unwittingly, foreshadows modern scholarly debates on this fresco, and on gender representation and ambiguity in Minoan iconography more generally, since no scholar, at that time, had seriously challenged the traditional and still popular interpretation of the two white-skinned figures in the Toreador fresco as being female (Momigliano, 2020: 6–7, figs. 1.3 and 1.4, with further references). More deliberately, the suggestion made by Thomas Burnett Swann in the 1960s that the Minoans wanted to conquer and dominate nature went against the grain of traditional views, which portrayed the Minoans as ante litteram flower-children living in harmony with the natural world, but seems to resonate with more recent interpretations of the 'naturalistic' Minoan iconography as evidence of domination of animals and their environment as well as a correlate of territorial expansion (cf. Section 5.2).

A fourth reason why Aegeomania contributes to Aegean Bronze Age studies is that it helps our understanding of public perceptions of this subject, and this could be important for the discipline's future. With this, I do not mean that one should pander to public taste in the hope of gaining popularity; rather, one should try to understand what can give Aegean Bronze Age archaeology new vitality and make us reflect upon our past, present, and future. In other words, specialists ignore at their own peril how different media have helped to disseminate their favourite subject to wide audiences and have given the Aegean Bronze Age relevance to the present. As acutely observed by Shapland (2021) in connexion with Minoan studies (and applicable to Aegean Bronze Age studies more generally), it appears that 'the more sophisticated archaeological theory became, the less cultural influence it had'. This is regrettable, since a fruitful study of the past should also be a dialogue with the present (cf. e.g. Finley, 1968: 7), and the study of Aegeomania can stimulate this conversation.

A fifth reason is that Aegeomania offers a case study, which can enhance our appreciation of the history of archaeology more broadly, and of changing popular views of this discipline. For example, nowadays archaeologists are often portrayed as athletic, globe-trotting heroes, who fight Nazis and crooks (as in the Indiana Jones film series), or as unsung heroes of humble origins, crushed by the

---

inspired by a transcendent presence, acting in freedom and restraint, unpurposeful as cyclic time itself' (Groenewegen-Frankfort, 1951: 216).

establishment and deserving more recognition (e.g. Basil Brown in John Preston's 2007 novel *The Dig* and in the 2021 film derived from it, directed by Simon Stone). Was this always the case? Aegeomanic works seem to suggest otherwise, as illustrated below by several examples (such as those by Gabriele D'Annunzio, Katharine Farrer, and Lawrence Durrell), and can help to provide us with a more nuanced view of the public's multifaceted and ever-changing relationship with archaeology.

2 In the Beginning: Aegeomania in the Late 19th Century (Early Belle Époque)

2.1 Prolegomena

Some Aegean Bronze Age monuments, such as the so-called Treasury of Atreus and Lion Gate at Mycenae (Figure 1), have remained largely visible since antiquity and were depicted in many works by architects and antiquarians

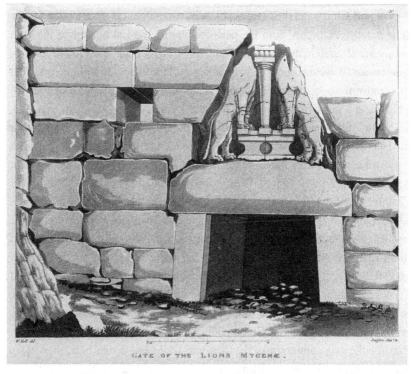

Figure 1 The Lion Gate at Mycenae in a drawing by William Gell (1810) (photo: https://commons.wikimedia.org/wiki/File: Gate_of_the_Lions_Mycenae_-_Gell_William_-_1810.jpg: work in the public domain).

who visited the Aegean in the 18th and 19th centuries (Blakolmer, 2010; Buscemi, 2010; Moore *et al.*, 2014; Driessen & Kalantzopoulou 2024; all with further references).

Their works, however, are arguably attempts to record these monuments rather than modern reimaginings of Aegean Bronze Age material culture as can be found in a poem or an abstract painting. Indeed, Aegeomanic works before Schliemann's excavations at Troy, Mycenae, and other Aegean Bronze Age sites in the 1870s–80s are very scarce: although further research may reveal others, the only clear example that I am aware of is the 1868 painting *Electra at the Tomb of Agamemnon* by Frederic Leighton, which refers to the relieving triangle of the Lion Gate at Mycenae (Figure 2, top right-hand corner), amid a quintessentially Neoclassical atmosphere.

2.2 Hellenizing Aegeomania (c. 1875–1900)

Although a widespread outbreak of Aegeomania occurred only after the redis-covery of Minoan culture in 1900, more instances of Aegeomanic works begin to appear after the watershed created by Schliemann's excavations in the 1870s. Some notable examples from the period covering the last quarter of the 19th century are attested in the visual arts and, like Leighton's *Electra at the Tomb of Agamemnon*, these incorporate Aegean Bronze Age elements within works that still conform to a lingering Neoclassical taste. Thus, representations of Schliemann's finds from Troy and Mycenae decorate his Athenian mansion, the 'Iliou Melathron', built for him by the German architect Ernst Ziller between 1878 and 1880, and these are embedded in larger compositions with an overall appearance of Italian Renaissance Classical revival, like the mansion itself (Darling, 2004: 155–8; Burns, 2010: 59–61; Pappalardo, 2021). For example, its mosaic floors show Trojan ceramic vessels and decorative motifs (e.g. Trojan swastikas) as well as Mycenaean jewellery, while one of the frescoes (by the Slovenian artist Jurij Šubic) depicts a group of putti, of whom one is holding a classical Greek theatrical mask and another a gold mask reminiscent of those found by Schliemann in the Shaft Graves of Mycenae (Figures 3, 4 and 5). As pointed out by Bryan Burns (2010: 59–61), we witness here the incorporation of Trojan and Mycenaean finds into the long continuum of Greek art and Greek history; and, one may add, their incorpor-ation into the long continuum of the Classical Tradition – a significant step in the process of Hellenization and Europeanization of the Aegean Bronze Age.

Two slightly later examples of this process are Schliemann's mausoleum in the First Cemetery in Athens (Figure 6), which was also designed by Ziller (Korres & Korres, 1981; Korres, 1984), and Franz von Matsch's painting *The*

Figure 2 Frederic Leighton: *Electra at the Tomb of Agamemnon*, c. 1868–9, oil on canvas (photo: https://commons.wikimedia.org/wiki/ File:1869_Frederic_Leighton_-_Electra_at_the_Tomb_of_Agamemnon.jpg, work in the public domain).

Triumph of Achilles (Figure 7), which is located in the Achilleion, the Neoclassical palace built by the Austro-Hungarian empress Elisabeth II on Corfu around 1889–92 (Blakolmer, 2006: 231, fig. 14.12; Kardamitsi-Adami, 2009: 247–65, fig. 338; Blakolmer, 2010;). In the mausoleum, allusions to Schliemann's Bronze Age finds are embedded in the friezes and metopes of a building that looks like a miniature Greek temple. In *The Triumph of Achilles*, the walls of Troy are represented with typical Bronze Age Cyclopean masonry, their gate is modelled on the Lion Gate at Mycenae (although the relieving triangle is decorated with a Trojan swastika instead of heraldic lions), while the

Figure 3 Overview of one of the reception rooms on the ground floor of
Schliemann's Athenian mansion, now housing the Numismatic Museum
(photo: N. Momigliano).

horse harnesses and Achilles' belt recall some gold finds from the Shaft Graves
at Mycenae.[7]

Allusions to the material culture of the Aegean Bronze Age appear also in
literary works of the last quarter of the 19th century, such as Emma Lazarus'
poem 'Agamemnon's Tomb' (1877) and Gabriele D'Annunzio's tragedy *La
città morta* (The Dead City) (Figure 8) as well as his largely autobiographical

---

[7] For Trojan swastikas see Schliemann (1875: esp. 12, 16, 39, 102, 107).

Figure 4 Detail of mosaic floor in Figure 3 (photo: N. Momigliano).

Figure 5 Detail of fresco with putti from Schliemann's Athenian mansion: one is holding a terracotta tragic mask and one a golden mask like those found by Schliemann in the Shaft Graves at Mycenae (photo: N. Momigliano).

Figure 6 Detail of frieze decorating Schliemann's mausoleum in the first cemetery in Athens (built c. 1892), showing Schliemann reading the *Iliad* to his wife, surrounded by workmen engaged in archaeological excavations as well as finds from Troy and other sites that he excavated (photo: N. Momigliano).

Figure 7 Franz von Matsch, *The Triumph of Achilles* (c. 1892) (photo http://commons.wikimedia.org/wiki/File:The_%22Triumph_of_Achilles%22_fresco,_in_Corfu_Achilleion.jpg).

novel *Il Fuoco* (The Flame), which includes a description of how D'Annunzio was inspired to write *La città morta* (D'Annunzio, 1899 and 1900).[8]

---

[8] A poem also titled 'Agamemnon's Tomb' was composed by the English poet and critic Sacheverell Sitwell (younger brother of Dame Edith Sitwell and Sir Osbert Sitwell), and first published in 1933; in turn, sections of Sitwell's poem were set to music by the British composer John Pickard between 2005–7, in a Requiem also titled 'Agamemnon's Tomb', first performed in 2008: https://research-information.bris.ac.uk/en/publications/agamemnons-tomb; https://john pickard.co.uk/works/choral/agamemnons-tomb-a-requiem/). *La città morta* had its first perform-ance in Paris in 1898 (in French), with Sarah Bernhardt in one of the main roles (the blind Anna);

Figure 8 Front cover of *L'Illustrazione Italiana* (24 March 1901) depicting a scene from the Italian premiere of D'Annunzio's *La città morta* (photo courtesy of Biblioteca di storia moderna e contemporanea, Roma).

the Italian premier was in Milan (1901), with the actress Eleonora Duse (also in the role of Anna): see e.g. Randi (2009). On some archaeological aspects of *La città morta* and *Il Fuoco* see Marabini Moevs (1985).

Lazarus, an American-Jewish poet most often remembered for her sonnet on the Statue of Liberty in New York ('The New Colossus'), was inspired by Schliemann's claim to have discovered the tombs of Agamemnon and his companions during his 1876 excavations at Mycenae. Only a year later, she published her poem 'Agamemnon's Tomb', expressing her amazement at the 'ponderous, golden mask of death' that is a 'worm-defying, uncorrupted lid' on the face of the dead hero, and also at the beauty of other 'precious relics', such as 'The golden buttons chased with wondrous craft' and 'The sheathed, bronze sword, the knife with brazen haft'. Her aesthetic appreciation of Schliemann's finds also spurred Lazarus to compare past and present and suggest that modern art only 'crudely apes' the 'grace' of the Bronze Age craftsmen, that the 'ancient majesty' of the heroic age dwarfs the 'puny semblance' of the present. Her immediate positive response, however, contrasts with that of some specialists, who did not initially believe that these finds were Greek (cf. 1 Introduction).

Great admiration for Schliemann's finds, but not for their excavator, also inspired D'Annunzio's *La città morta*, composed soon after the Italian author visited Greece in 1895. This works interweaves Greek mythology and Aegean Bronze Age material culture, as illustrated by D'Annunzio's precise references (and allusions) both to Attic tragedies and to Schliemann's Mycenaean finds.[9] *La città morta* is a revival of a Classical literary genre, but its Nietzschean and psychological elements give this tragedy a much more modern, and modernist, flavour than the serene Neoclassical reimaginings of the Aegeomanic frescoes, mosaics, and paintings described above. D'Annunzio's dead (and deadly) city is Mycenae, where the action takes place. One of the characters is the archaeologist Leonardo, whose increasingly erratic behaviour culminates in sororicide, after he excavates the tombs of Agamemnon, Cassandra, and their companions. His febrile search for and excavation of their graves turn out to be partly an attempt to suppress his incestuous urges towards his sister. Archaeology, however, does not offer a remedy: the excavated earth emanates 'vapours of the monstrous faults' committed by the Atreids, and the dead people Leonardo is looking for 'are resurrected inside him violently and exhale inside him the dreadful spirit that Aeschylus instilled in them'.[10] He murders his sister to preserve her purity and extinguish his carnal desires.

The character of Leonardo seems partly to represent the archaeologist's attempt to be a Nietzschean Übermensch (superman or overman), whose extraordinary discovery of the Mycenaean graves and finds makes past and present

---

[9] See especially the descriptions of the objects in Act 1, Scene 5, and in Act 2, scenes 1 and 2. Interestingly, however, D'Annunzio, following Homer and disregarding Schliemann's reports, places the remains of the dead inside cremation urns.

[10] See dialogues in Act 1, Scene 4 (my English translation from the original Italian).

collide, turns myth into history, and history into myth.[11] He is, however, a flawed Übermensch, as elaborated in *Il Fuoco*. In this novel, the main character (the fictional author Stelio Éffrena, who is partly based on D'Annunzio) recounts how, during a visit to Mycenae, he was inspired to write a modern tragedy, and describes the plot of *La città morta*. He also mentions his regret that the 'esploratore barbarico' (barbaric explorer), the 'grosso Schliemann' (crass Schliemann), a businessman who spent much of his life in a drugstore, had made such amazing discoveries, and expresses his wish that, instead, the tombs had been found by 'uno spirito giovenile e fervente . . . un poeta . . . un animatore' (a young and fervid spirit, a poet, a life-giver) (D'Annunzio, 1900: 290–1). In other words, *La città morta* could be seen as an attempt to take the discovery of the Shaft Graves of Mycenae to a higher level of meaning, which only a poet and life-giver like D'Annunzio could achieve. This finds an echo in Oscar Wilde's idea (first published in 1885) that:

> archaeology is only really delightful when transfused into some form of art. I have no desire to underrate the services of the laborious scholars, but I feel that the use Keats made of Lemprière's Dictionary is of far more value to us than Professor Max Müller's treatment of the same mythology as a disease of language. Better *Endymion* than any theory, however sound, or, as in the present instance, unsound, of an epidemic among adjectives! And who does not feel that the chief glory of Piranesi's book on vases is that it gave Keats the suggestion for his "Ode on a Grecian Urn"? Art, and art only, can make archaeology beautiful. (Wilde, 2003: 1163)[12]

Whether D'Annunzio's *La città morta* makes archaeology 'delightful' and is a significant improvement on Schliemann's own mythologizing narratives is debatable.[13] It is clear, however, that one finds here an early example of a literary *topos* that will reappear in other Aegeomanic works: the Aegean Bronze Age archaeologist not as a hero, that is as some ante litteram Indiana Jones, but as the bad guy – a very flawed, conceited Übermensch, who makes past and present collide, but also steals finds, is economical with the truth, blurs

---

[11] On the archaeologist Leonardo as Übermensch see e.g. Act 1, Scene 5: ' . . . Se hai veduto veramente quel che tu dici, tu non se più un uomo' (If you have really seen what you say, you are no longer a man). Marabini Moevs (1985: 67–70) suggests that Leonardo is a flawed archaeologist also because, in D'Annunzio's tragedy, he incarnates the Neoplatonic conceptions of Winckelmann that were rejected by the Italian poet. On Schliemann, Evans, and Aegean archaeology vis-a-vis Nietzsche's idea of the Übermensch see also Gere (2009: esp. Chapters 1 and 2, and p. 36).

[12] Passage taken from the essay 'The truth of masks: a note on illusion', first published in 1885 in the British monthly magazine *The Nineteenth Century* as 'Shakespeare and Stage Costume' (see Wilde, 2003: 1247).

[13] On Schliemann's own mythologizing (i.e., his ability to embellish his own life and discoveries) see e.g. Traill (1995); Easton (1998); Runnels (2007); Traill (2014).

authenticity and fakery, and even commits murder. Besides D'Annunzio's *La città morta* this is illustrated, for example, by Katharine Farrer's 1954 detective novel *The Cretan Counterfeit*, Lawrence Durrell's psychological novel *Cefalù* (first published in 1947, and later republished in 1958 with the title *The Dark Labyrinth*), and Ackroyd's above-mentioned novel *The Fall of Troy* (where, surely not by chance, the author substitutes the surname Schliemann with 'Obermann' – a German surname deriving from the words meaning 'upper' or 'above' and 'man').[14]

3 Aegeomania in the Late Belle Époque (c. 1900–1914): the Emergence of the Cretomania Variant

As I hinted above, a veritable outbreak of Aegeomania started only after 1900, and this was largely in the form of the virulent Cretomania variant. This was caused by the discoveries made by Evans and other archaeologists from 1900 onwards on Crete and revived an interest in the Aegean Bronze Age more generally.

Some very early examples of this outbreak are attested in haute couture and vernacular architecture, as illustrated by the 'Knossos' scarves (Figure 9) created by Mariano Fortuny y Madrazo in 1906 (Caloi, 2011 and 2017), and the villa (now destroyed) that the photographer Bahaettin Rahmi Bediz built in 1904 in an olive grove near Heraklion (Figure 10), and was designed by the Danish artist Halvor Bagge (who had worked for Evans at Knossos between 1902 and 1905).[15] This is possibly the very first example of a 'Neo-Minoan' style in architecture or, to use Osbert Lancaster's phrase, 'that okapi among architectural modes, Minoan Revival' (Lancaster, 1947: 70–1; see also Cadogan, 2004: figs. 49.2 and 49.3; Momigliano, 2020: 76).

Besides, several intriguing examples of Aegeomania appear in theatrical productions. In the last quarter of the 19th century – after Schliemann's finds at Troy and Mycenae of the 1870s but before Evans' work at Knossos in 1900 –

---

[14] On Farrer's and Durrell's novels, see also Momigliano (2020: 155–7) and Momigliano (2021: 307–11), respectively. There are many Aegeomanic books in which archaeologists are heroic figures, but these tend to be later in date and seem to betray the influence of the Indiana Jones franchise and Dan Brown's *The Da Vinci Code* (2003). Examples of Aegeomanic thrillers with dashing archaeologists are Gavin Scott's trilogy *Age of Treachery* (2016), *Age of Olympus* (2017), and *Age of Exodus* (2018) and some of the volumes in David Gibbins' series featuring the fictional marine archaeologist Jack Howard, such as *Atlantis* (2005) and *The Mask of Troy* (2010). Scott's novels are inspired by the history of Minoan archaeological research and feature a fictional Oxford don, Duncan Forrester, who gets tantalizingly close, but never quite manages to decipher an important Minoan inscription.

[15] A document in Ottoman Turkish in the Vikelaia Library in Heraklion, written by Bahaettin Rahmi Bediz, indicates that the idea of using a Neo-Minoan style for the villa was Bagge's, who also supervised its construction. I am grateful to Irem Yildiz (St Antony's College, Oxford), for her translation of this document.

Figure 9 Mariano Fortuny's portrait of his wife (c. 1935) wearing one of the 'Knossos' scarves that he started producing in 1906 and a dress decorated with Minoan motifs, Fortuny Museum, Venice (photo: N. Momigliano).

there were many performances of Greek drama in numerous countries, but only very few used the material culture of the Aegean Bronze Age, such as the *Antigone* staged by the Comédie Française in 1893 (Giannouli, 2012) and the *Agamemnon* staged by the University of Cambridge in 1900, which used reproductions of the Lion Gate at Mycenae as one of their stage-props.[16] Most productions of Greek dramas before 1900, however, continued to adopt a classicizing look, such as the *Agamemnon* staged in Oxford on 3 June 1880, with sets by Burne-Jones and costumes by W. B Richmond, and George Warr's

---

[16] For the Lion Gate in the 1900 Cambridge production of *Agamemnon* see www.cambridgegreek play.com/plays/1900/agamemnon and www.apgrd.ox.ac.uk/productions/production/831.

Figure 10 Sketch of Neo-Minoan villa by H. Bagge, created for the photographer Bahaettin Rahmi Bediz in 1904 (courtesy of the Vikelaia Library, Heraklion).

1882 *Tale of Troy* (Macintosh, 1997: 291–2), and many other performances by the Comédie Française of the 1890s (according to Sideris, 1976: 181). In 1901, however, the Greek theatrical company Nea Skini staged a production of Euripides' *Alcestis* in Athens, which was described as innovative partly because of its 'Minoan' appearance (Sideris, 1976: 181). An image of this production illustrated by Sideris (1976: 144, fig. 9) shows the entrance of Admetus' palace as a portico with tapering columns and stone friezes decorated with spirals. This is largely modelled on architectural and decorative elements of the so-called Treasury of Atreus and palace at Mycenae (cf. illustrations in Perrot & Chipiez, 1894), which excavations at Knossos, in particular, had shown to be ultimately derived from Minoan Crete.

Nea Skini's production of *Alcestis* started the new trend of using Aegean Bronze Age elements, especially 'Minoan', in the sets and costumes of modern performances of Classical Greek drama and of other works (e.g. ballets, book illustrations, films) inspired by Greek mythological narratives more generally. This trend continued throughout the late Belle Époque and has continued uninterrupted up to the present century as shown, for example, by the very Minoan production of Mozart's *Idomeneo* by Opera San Jose in

2011 and by the many Aegean Bronze Age elements in the 2018 BBC/ Netflix series *Troy: Fall of a City*.[17]

The use of Aegean Bronze Age motifs suited the contemporary Art Nouveau's reaction against classicism and the fashion for primitivism. It also allowed authors and artists to show their learning, their up-to-date knowledge of the latest archaeological discoveries, and their striving for authenticity, since their Aegeomania indicated their awareness that their stories, dramas, operas, ballets and other works were inspired by ancient Greek narratives, which were set in a distant, heroic past going back to the 2nd millennium BC, not in 5th century BC Athens. Examples of this are Richard Strauss' opera *Elektra* (1909), Max Reinhardt's London production of *Oedipus Rex* (1912), and Bakst's costumes and sets for various ballets and dramas of the 1910s (Figure 11), including some of his creations for the company founded by Sergei Diaghilev, the Ballets Russes, such as *Narcisse, Daphne and Chloe*, and *L'Après-midi d'un Faune* (Momigliano, 2017b). The quest for modernity and authenticity was explicitly recognized by these artists or by people closely connected with their productions. For example, Bakst stated that Minoan art felt close and familiar, and he wanted to show in his sets and costumes the Homeric world as he saw it, after he had conducted research on Crete, which he had visited in 1907 (Momigliano, 2017b). Similarly, Gilbert Murray, the Regius Professor of Greek at the University of Oxford, who had produced the English translation for Reinhardt's London production of *Oedipus Rex*, defended the latter's use of Minoan–Mycenaean elements in the performance because the supposed date of the Oedipus story did not belong to Classical Athens, but the Bronze Age Aegean (Momigliano, 2020: 83, with further references).

Sometimes, however, the use of Aegean Bronze Age elements stemmed more pointedly from socio-political reasons. This is the case of the 1909 drama *La Furie* by Henri Jules Bois, which was loosely inspired by Euripides' *The Madness of Heracles*. The feminist Jules Bois used Minoan costumes created by Désiré Chaineux (Figure 12) in the first production of this work because he wanted to bring the recent discoveries on Crete to a wider public, and this was prompted by his belief that the Minoans had established a form of collectivism and feminism that could be a model for contemporary European society. This was an interesting elaboration of Evans' ideas on the importance of women in Minoan Crete (and the existence of some form of matriarchy in the early stages of Minoan history), and of Angelo Mosso's suggestion that the Minoan palaces

---

[17] For the Opera San Jose's production of *Idomeneo* (which was supported by the philanthropist David Packard, who has a life-long interest in ancient Greece and Minoan Crete), see www.shomler.com/ osj/idomeneo/index.htm and https://manhattan.institute/article/idomeneo-on-crete; For *Troy: Fall of a City, see* www.netflix.com/gb/title/80175352.

Figure 11 Bakst's set design for the stage production of Émile Verhaeren's
Hélène de Sparte (1912), showing several Aegean Bronze Age elements
(e.g. Lion Gate, Minoan columns); the faces carved on the rocks recall both the
famous gold masks from the Shaft Graves at Mycenae and the painted plaster
head found by Tsountas, also at Mycenae, in 1896. Paris, National Museum of
Modern Art, Pompidou centre (https://www.centrepompidou.fr/fr/ressources/
oeuvre/cx454q; see also https://commons.wikimedia.org/wiki/Category:
Helene_de_Sparte_(Bakst)#/media/File:Helene_de_Sparte_ballet
_by_L._Bakst_01.jpg).

were destroyed by a great revolution 'in which Socialism triumphed' (Mosso,
1907: 163; see also Momigliano, 2020: 82–3, with further references). Indeed,
the popularity of the Minoans in the early 20th century and in subsequent
periods is also largely due to the fact that feminist interpretations of this ancient
culture resonated with modern issues, such as the 'Woman Question' during the
first feminist wave, and they have continued to resonate with the issues highlighted by later feminist waves. For many people the idea that Minoan Crete was
a matriarchy is among its most appealing traits, a source of hope and inspiration.
Whether this reflects an ancient reality or modern desires, however, is a matter
of opinion.

　　These productions of *La Furie*, *Elektra*, and *Oedipus Rex* are intriguing also
because they show an interest in mental disorders and the psychopathology of
sexual desires, which betrays the growing influence of the great Parisian

Figure 12 Sketch of 'Minoan' costume by Désiré Chaineux (1851–1919, designer at the Comédie Française from 1897–1919, specializing in historical creations). This was created for Jules Bois' drama *La Furie* (1909) and was displayed at the 2014 exhibition *La Grèce des origins: entre rêve et archéologie*, Musée d'Archéologie Nationale, Châteu Saint-Germain-en-Laye, Paris (photo: N. Momigliano).

neurologist, Jean-Martin Charcot, and of one of his most famous pupils, Sigmund Freud, the founder of psychoanalysis, and arguably one of the most famous sufferers from Aegeomania. Freud was fascinated by archaeology and a keen collector of antiquities (see e.g. Armstrong, 2005; Burke, 2006a, 2006b),[18] and his collection included some Aegean Bronze Age (Mycenaean) materials (D'Agata, 1994). He followed closely the discoveries made by Schliemann and

---

[18] See also the 2023 exhibition at the Freud Museum in London: https://stories.freud.org.uk/freuds-antiquity-object-idea-desire/).

Evans, referred to them in his own publications, and in the 1930s he even produced a Minoan diagnosis for one of his patients, as discussed below (Section 4.2).

4 Aegeomania and World Wars (c. 1914–1945)

4.1 Overview

The period that the Marxist historian Eric Hobsbawm (1994) dubbed 'the age of catastrophes' (c. 1914–45) saw many Aegeomanic developments, including the emergence of another variant: 'Cycladomania'. In this period, specialist and non-specialist works often portray Minoans and Mycenaeans in opposite, binary terms, such as feminine vs masculine, decadent vs vigorous, and non-Aryan vs Aryan. This perspective was largely influenced by the growth of Aryanism and the idea that Minoans and Mycenaeans belonged to different races.[19] It was also helped by the fact that Evans' quasi-monotheistic interpretation of Minoan religion as centred on the worship of a supreme Mother Goddess had reached an almost canonical status, despite some dissenting views. This, in turn, encouraged the perception of the Minoans as non-Aryan, since the linguistic evidence linked the Indo-Europeans with the worship of a supreme male deity presiding over a pantheon of male and female divinities – and the Mycenaeans were often identified with the Indo-European Homeric Achaeans well before the decipherment of Linear B.[20]

In the interwar period, Aegeomania continued to appear in many works of literature, and now in a wider array of genres – from historical novels to epic poetry, travel writing, and even Mills & Boon romances, such as Nigel Worth's *The Arms of Phaedra: A Tale of Wonder and Adventure* (1924), which also illustrates the popularity of some notions about Minoan religion, proto-feminism, and alleged female forward sexuality (Momigliano, 2020: 124). Aegeomania continued to appear also in the visual and performing arts, and even in upmarket home furnishings, as illustrated by the textiles designed by Josef Frank for Svenskt Tenn, a leading Swedish interior design company founded in 1924 in Stockholm by Estrid Ericson (Figures 13–14; for another

---

[19] This binary view of Minoans/Mycenaeans was not shared by some scholars, especially by Evans. According to him, the Mycenaeans were not Greeks, but were simply an offshoot of the Minoans, and Greek-speaking northern tribes had entered the Aegean only around 1200 BC (and destroyed the Minoan–Mycenaean palaces). Evans' view, however, was already becoming obsolete in the interwar period, even before the decipherment of Linear B showed beyond reasonable doubt that Greek was already spoken in the Aegean well before 1200 BC (cf. Momigliano, 2020: 140, with further references).

[20] Cf. note 19.

Figure 13 Samples of two versions of the textile fabric 'Anakreon' created by Josef Frank for Svenskt Tenn in 1938, in possession of the author (photo N. Momigliano; copyright of fabric: Svenskt Tenn, Stockholm).

Figure 14 'Blue Bird' fresco, Knossos (after Evans, 1928: 454, colour plate XI).

example of interwar Aegeomanic interior furnishings see Boucher, 2017). One of the most intriguing cases, however, is that of Freudian psychoanalysis, as described below.

4.2 Freud's Minoan Psychoanalysis

As shown by Cathy Gere (2009:153–71), in the spring of 1933 the imagist poet H.D. (Hilda Doolittle) travelled to Vienna to be treated by Freud, and the famous psychoanalyst provided her with a Minoan diagnosis. After some sessions, he suggested to H.D. that her poetical obsession with Greek islands and things Minoan, as well as her neurosis, hallucinations, and bisexuality were symptoms of her regression to a pre-Oedipal, mother-fixated layer in her psyche. According to Freud's controversial theory of inherited memory, this pre-Oedipal layer was connected with the Mother Goddess-matriarchal stage in the evolution of European history, which corresponded to the Minoan period. As Gere (2006: 217) has pointed out, however, the acceptance of the idea of a Minoan Mother Goddess and Minoan matriarchy may suggest that 'when it came to reading Evans, Freud himself was not Freudian enough' and that, perhaps, he should have 'diagnosed the archaeologist as mother-fixated' instead, something that may have been partly caused by the death of his mother when he was a child of six.

One can debate whether the loss of his own mother greatly influenced Evans' vision of Minoan religion as dominated by a maternal figure (see also MacGillivray, 2000: 193; Lapatin, 2002: 67; Morris, 2006: 73). My own view is that previous scholarship on Greek religion and social evolution, especially the works of the so-called Cambridge Ritualists, was equally if not more significant in shaping Evans' ideas (see e.g. Momigliano, 2020: 60, with further bibliography). At any rate, the consequences of Evans' Mother Goddess-fixation are considerable, since they have affected many generations of specialists and non-specialists alike. The corpus of scholarly and Aegeomanic works of all periods that associate the Minoans with a supreme female deity (and, if not with matriarchy, at least with the notion that Minoan women had considerable status in society) is considerable and continues to grow, largely because, as mentioned above, this has been a source of hope and inspiration to many people. In the interwar period, however, the allegedly proto-feminist and feminine Minoans came to be perceived as decadent and, by contrast, the Mycenaeans as masculine, vigorous barbarians.

4.3 Feminine, Decadent Minoans vs Masculine, Vigorous Mycenaeans

Among some early examples of this trend are two universal histories: *The Decline of the West* (1918–22) by Oswald Spengler, and the *Outline of History* (1920) by H. G. Wells. These two works, now almost forgotten, are good illustrations of the *fin de siècle*'s preoccupation with decadence (which resurged after World War I), and both were influential bestsellers in the interwar period, especially Spengler's. In his *Decline of the West*, the Minoans are compared to decadent late Romans, pampered in luxury; they are Oriental and contemptuous of less civilized peoples. By contrast, the Mycenaeans are likened to 'healthy barbarians', gifted with the 'bearish morning vigour of the German lands' (Spengler, 1928: 87–9). In a similar vein, H. G. Wells described Minoan achievements as overrated, was suspicious of their alleged pacifism, and considered their eventual conquest and absorption by the Greeks ('a healthy barbaric Aryan people') as a well-deserved fate (Wells, 1920: 214–15).[21]

Decadent Minoans and vigorous Mycenaeans appear also in many other literary genres, such as historical novels, of which a good example is *Gyðjan og uxinn: skáldsaga* (The Goddess and the Bull: A Novel) by the Icelandic author Kristmann Gudmundsson (1937; translated into English as *Winged Citadel* in 1940). This work tells the story of a youth from Macedonia, who migrates to Crete and becomes the main Cretan ruler or 'Minos' thanks to his marriage to the sovereign Minoan queen. In the novel, the Minoans are described as a 'gentle and decadent race, bred in a humane, civilized atmosphere' (Gudmundsson, 1940: 408), and very vulnerable to military attacks. By contrast, the Mycenaeans/ Achaeans represent the idea that might is right, and they are the future: 'The Mycenaeans, rising in might and splendor . . . this was the Future on the march!' (Gudmundsson, 1940: 407). The Minoan decline and the growing Mycenaean power culminate with the fall of Knossos, which appears in the novel as a prefiguration of the fall of Troy – an early round on the conquering path of the Mycenaeans, who are equated with the Homeric Achaeans. Gudmundsson's Mycenaeans launch an attack on Knossos with a fleet of 'about a thousand ships', which can be read as an allusion to the famous verses 'Was this the face that launch'd a thousand ships, / And burnt the topless towers of Ilium' in Christopher Marlowe's Elizabethan tragedy *Doctor Faustus* (Act V, Scene I, when Faust conjures the ghost of Helen; this in turn, alludes to the famous catalogue of ships in book 2 of the *Iliad*). Indeed, in the novel the fall of Knossos appears to prefigure not only the fall of Troy, but also the turmoil of interwar Europe, and the rise of fascist movements. Drawing on some archaeological and other narratives that had become dominant in the interwar period, and on his own inventiveness, Gudmundsson presents Minoan Crete as a pacifist, matriarchal, and sexually liberated society that in the second half of the 2nd millennium BC succumbed to the patriarchal and warlike Mycenaeans. While the narrator/author admired the gender equality and sexual mores of the Minoans, he believed that Minoan society had become over-refined and decadent. Above all, he felt that the

---

[21] On the myth of Minoan pacifism, the origins of which are often (wrongly) attributed to Evans, see Momigliano (2020: 65–9).

Minoans' extreme liberalism and pacifism paved the way for their downfall, since they allowed the flourishing of extremist factions and made Knossos vulnerable to the attacks of war-like people.

Dissolute, decadent Minoans defeated by, or with the help of, healthy Aryan tribes on the rise loom large also in poetry and children's books. For example, they appear in the already mentioned epic poem *The Odyssey: a Modern Sequel* by Kazantzakis (1938; 1958), an author much influenced by Spengler's ideas.[22] In this work, Kazantzakis portrayed the fall of Knossos as a prefiguration of the Bolshevik storming of the Winter Palace, and the Minoan elite as a prefiguration of the decadent Western bourgeoisie and aristocracy of the late 19th–early 20th century.[23] Among children's books, examples of this trend are *At the Palace of Knossos*, also by Kazantzakis (published posthumously in 1988, but written around 1940), and *The Winged Girl of Knossos*, published in 1933 by Erick Berry (nom de plume of Allena Champlin). Both are modern retellings of ancient Greek mythological narratives (Theseus and the Minotaur; the flight of Daedalus and Icarus), which make extensive use of Minoan archaeology to provide local colour and a more 'authentic' chronological setting, with an added feminist twist in the case of Berry's version, which has a female heroine.

In the context of rising Aryanism, it is not surprising to find portrayals of decadent Minoans and vigorous Mycenaeans, especially in universal histories and modern retellings of the myth of Theseus and the Minotaur, which had long been used as a metaphor for the Hellenic Mycenaean conquest of the non-Hellenic Minoan world. Yet, in the interwar period, negative perceptions of the Minoans appear also in other genres, such as travel writing, and in works by very different authors, from Jacques de Lacretelle, to Camille Mauclair, Mario Praz, and Evelyn Waugh.[24] Mauclair, for example, in his *Le pur visage de la Grèce* described his first impression of Knossos as a place that is dead and does not inspire emotions, largely because he found Evans' reconstructions unpleasant and reminiscent of modern garages and pavilions in colonial exhibitions (Mauclair, 1934: 232–5) – perhaps a reference to the *Exposition Coloniale Internationale* held in Paris in 1931. Even if some finds in the Heraklion Museum produced more positive reactions, Mauclair had many reservations

---

[22] On Spengler's influence on Kazantzakis and his *Odyssey* see e.g. González-Vaquerizo (2021) (with further references); on the Minoans in the works of Kazantzakis in general see Beaton (2006) and (2008).

[23] In Kazantzakis' *The Odyssey*, the fall of Knossos is caused by an uprising of slaves helped by the Dorians (rather than Mycenaeans) and led by one of Idomeneus' daughters. This may suggest that Kazantzakis as late as 1938 was still following Evans' interpretation of the Aegean Bronze Age, according to which the Mycenaeans were not Greeks, but merely an offshoot of the Minoans, whereas Greek speaking northern tribes (the Dorians) entered the Aegean only around 1200 BC and destroyed the Minoan–Mycenaean palaces (cf. note 19).

[24] For more examples of Minoan decadence in the interwar period see Momigliano (2020: 104–18).

about others: he is effusive about the modernity of Minoan frescoes and writes admiringly of Minoan stone vases (which he compares to works by Antoine Bourdelle and Antoine-Louis Barye), but he describes the famous faience 'snake goddess' figurines as disturbing and comic at the same time, while his overall conclusion about Minoan art is that it is far too remote to provoke emotions; he is happy to return to Athens and its Acropolis (Mauclair, 1934: 245–50). Mauclair is more impressed by the ruins of Mycenae, which he describes as majestic and fascinating, expressing an intriguing savage barbarity, evocative of the Vandals and Medieval times (Mauclair, 1934: 199, 251) – ideas that remind one, once again, of Spengler's views.

4.4 Earthy and Worldly Minoans vs Cruel and Violent Mycenaeans

In the interwar period the opposition between Minoan and Mycenaeans did not create views of the former that were only negative and decadent. On the contrary, among some authors, Minoan Crete became a Garden of Eden full of sexual promise, a lost paradise that was also a hope for the future. For example, D.H. Lawrence, in his poem 'The Middle of the World', presents the 'slim naked men from Cnossus' as people from a distant, idealized, and sensual past, but also as the future, because they smile the 'archaic smile of those that will without fail come back again' (Lawrence, 2002: 575).[25] Perhaps the most emblematic expression of a passionate reception of the Minoans in this period appears in Henry Miller's *Colossus of Maroussi*, which recounts his stay in Greece on the eve of World War II. For Miller, the virtues of Minoan Crete are encapsulated by the sites of Phaistos and, above all, Knossos. His Minoans are modern, sane, healthy, egalitarian, down to earth, carefree, opulent, powerful, and peaceful; Phaistos 'contained all the elements of the heart' and was 'femin- ine through and through', while 'Knossos was worldly in the best sense of the word' (Miller, 1941: 121–2, 150). By contrast, his Mycenaeans are more paradoxical. In Miller's words, at Mycenae 'gods once walked the earth', but 'everything about the place is contradictory ... grim, lovely, seductive and repellent' at the same time, while 'Tiryns smells of cruelty, barbarism, suspi- cion, isolation. It is like an H. G. Wells setting for a prehistoric drama, for a thousand years' war between one-eyed giants and blunder-footed dinosaurs' (Miller, 1941: 85–6).[26]

One suspects that this grim and contradictory vision is partly due to the fact that it is difficult to disentangle the ruins of Mycenae from the stories of

---

[25] Composed around 1930 and published posthumously (see Momigliano, 2020: 120, with note 161 and further bibliography).

[26] For more examples of Minoan Crete as Garden of Eden in the interwar period, see Momigliano (2020: 118–24).

betrayal, adultery, murder, cannibalism, incest, and rape that have come down to us from Classical authors – as indeed shown in *La città morta* by D'Annunzio and in many later works, such as the poem 'Mycenae', composed in the interwar period by Giorgos Seferis (who was a friend of Miller and the first Greek writer to become a Nobel laureate). In this poem, the great stones of Mycenae (Figure 1) evoke the poet's own experience of cycles of murder and revenge, like those portrayed in Aeschylus' *Oresteia*, as well as the burdensome ancient past that modern Greeks must bear:

> Sinks whoever raises the great stones sinks;
> I've raised these stones as long as I was able
> I've loved these stones as long as I was able
> these stones, my fate.
> Wounded by my own soil
> tortured by my own shirt
> condemned by my own gods,
> these stones.
>
> I know that they don't know, but I
> who've followed so many times
> the path from killer to victim
> from victim to punishment
> from punishment to the next murder,
> groping
> the inexhaustible purple
> that night of the return
> when the Furies began whistling
> in the meagre grass
> (Seferis 2018, English translation by E. Keeley and P. Sherrard).[27]

To return, however, to the connection between the Minoans, the feminine, and the Orient (vs the connection between the Mycenaeans, the masculine, and the West), this also extends to other cultural practices, from the visual to the performing arts. A striking example of this is Ted Shawn's dance 'Gnossienne', first performed in 1919. As illustrated by Christine Morris (2017), this dance, rich in allusions to Minoan material culture, was set to music by Eric Satie, and represented a Minoan priest performing a ritual at the altar of the 'snake goddess'. It was usually presented in the 'Oriental' section

---

[27] Also available at https://allpoetry.com/poem/14330740-Ii.-Mycenae-by-Giorgos-Seferis. Another poem by Seferis related to the archaeology of the Aegean Bronze Age is 'The king of Asine', which links a visit to the archaeological site with a line from the *Iliad*. This poem, like 'Mycenae', tackles the theme of the burdensome Classical past, but also evokes the idea that the Aegean Bronze Age is distant and unknowable, since the king of Asine is 'a void under the mask' (www.poetryfoun dation.org/poems/51356/the-king-of-asini).

of the Denishawn Dancers repertoire (the company founded by Shawn with his wife, the famous dancer Ruth St Denis), and was a tribute to the idea of a dominant female Minoan deity. In addition, the dance could be read as a comment on (and resistance to) the dominance of females in modern dance at that time.[28]

4.5 From Poetry to Dramas and Movies: Minoans, Mycenaeans, and Trojans

The use of Aegean Bronze Age elements in the sets and costumes of modern theatrical performances inspired by Greek mythological narratives continued in the interwar period. Three examples of this are: Ida Rubinstein's *Phédre*, a multi-media production of D'Annunzio's 1909 tragedy *Fedra*, performed in Paris in 1923, with music by Ildebrando Pizzetti and sets and costumes by Bakst, arguably the most Cretomanic work ever produced by this Russian artist (Figure 15); the modernist staging of Euripides' *Medea* directed by Otte Sköld in 1934 at the Royal Dramatic Theatre in Stockholm, with Swedish translation by Hjalmar Gullberg and Minoan-style costumes (Figure 16); and the production of Racine's *Phèdre* by Jean-Louis Barrault at the Comédie Française in

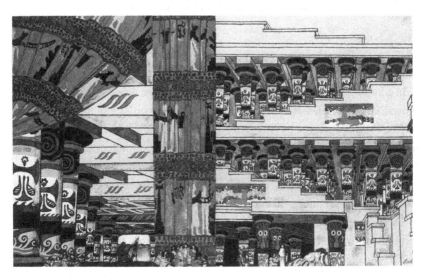

Figure 15 Bakst's sketch for *Phédre*, Ida Rubinstein's multimedia production of D'Annunzio *Fedra*, staged in Paris in 1923 (https://commons.wikimedia.org/wiki/File:Phaedra_(Bakst)_01.jpg)

---

[28] Shawn's protégée, Barton Mumaw, also performed 'Gnossienne' in the 1930s (Morris, 2017: 111).

SVENSKA DAGBLADET

Söndagen den 18 Februari 1934

Inför Dramatens Medea-premiär — säsongens stora evenemang

Dramatiska teaterns premiär på torsdag, då Euripides' antika drama för första gången går över svensk scen, gör anspråk på att rubriceras som en av teatersäsongens stora händelser. Olof Molander svarar för den i mer än ett hänseende märkliga iscensättningen, som bland annat kommer att bjuda på en del överraskande scentekniska nyheter. Professor Otte Sköld har komponerat den dekorativa ramen och de praktfulla dräkterna, som ge prov på den kretensiska kulturens rikedom i färg och originalitet i mönster, och några av teaterns främsta krafter återfinnas i personalförteckningen med Tora Teje i spetsen som Medea, Edvin Adolphson som Jason, Ivar Kåge som Aigeus, Sven Bergvall som Kreon och Renée Björling som ledarinnan av den kvinnliga kören. Vi hänvisa för övrigt till artikel på annan plats.

Figure 16 Newspaper cutting (*Svenska Dagbladet*) reporting on Otte Sköld's 1934 production of Euripides' *Medea* at the Royal Dramatic Theatre in Stockholm (photo N. Momigliano, reproduced by courtesy of the Archive of the Royal Dramatic Theatre in Stockholm).

1942, with Jean Hugo's classicizing sets juxtaposed to costumes based on Minoan dress (Humbert-Mougin, 2006).

In addition, in this period the use of Aegean Bronze Age elements extends to films. Early examples of this are some silent movies on Trojan themes, such as *Helena* (1924), directed by Manfred Noa, which used a replica of the Knossian throne as the symbol of Priam's royalty and power.[29] Another example is *The Private Life of Helen of Troy* (1927), directed by Alexander Korda, in which one of Helen's alluring dresses is embroidered with Minoan sprays of lilies, in combination with more classicizing features (Momigliano, 2020: 130, fig. 4.13a). These two silent films anticipate the more extensive use of Minoan material culture to be found in later movies about Troy, such as *Helen of Troy* (1956) directed by Robert Wise,[30] Wolfgang Petersen's *Troy* (2004), starring

---

[29]   Christian C. Schnell, 'The career of an archaeological object in the movies. The "Throne of Minos" as requisite and icon in *Helena* (1924) and *La Guerra di Troia* (1961)', paper presented at the conference 'Replica knowledge: histories, processes and identities', 2-4 February 2017, Berlin (Humboldt University): https://wissenschaftliche-sammlungen.de/files/4314/8412/7119/Replica-Knowledge-Program.pdf ; see also Winkler (2007: 204) and www.edition-filmmuseum.com/product_info.php/language/en/info/p163_Helena–Der-Untergang-Trojas.html.

[30]   See www.imdb.com/title/tt0049301/; www.themoviedb.org/movie/42658-helen-of-troy.

Brad Pitt as Achilles, and even in the BBC/Netflix production of the 8-episode series *Troy: Fall of a City* (2018). In Wise's film Troy almost looks like Minoan Knossos (Nisbet, 2006: 31–6; Winkler, 2007: 206; Winkler, 2015: 19); in Petersen's film the use of Minoan elements is more moderate, but even in his version the Trojan buildings (like those of Wise's film) are provided with Minoan 'horns of consecration' (see also below). In the BBC/Netflix series, Minoan columns, frescoes, and objects appear in almost every episode, and are particularly common in king Priam's abode.

This assimilation of Minoan elements in modern reimaginings of Troy and the Trojans from the early 20th century to the present may, at first, appear rather puzzling[31] (at least to Aegean Bronze Age specialists) but can perhaps be explained in terms of aesthetic, practical, and historiographical reasons, as follows.

Regarding aesthetic and practical reasons, as already mentioned, in the early 20th century Minoan Crete was rapturously received by the artistic avant-gardes of several European cities, and their use of Minoan elements effectively became a way of providing some historical authenticity for stories, dramas, ballets, and operas set chronologically in pre-Classical Greece, even if these did not have a specific Cretan content. This popularity paved the way for the incorporation of Minoan elements into Trojan contexts, especially when artists/writers identified the Homeric Achaeans with the Mycenaean Greeks and wanted to show the Trojan as a distinct but also contemporary culture of the Aegean Bronze Age. But why did they not use more specifically Trojan elements? Here practical issues may come into play: even after Carl Blegen's well-known excavations at Troy in the 1930s, and their subsequent publication in several volumes in the 1950s (e.g. Blegen *et al.*, 1950; Blegen *et al.*, 1958), the books and illustrations available did not offer much that could easily spark the imagination of film directors and people involved in creating the sets: although Troy could boast remarkable fortification walls, unlike Knossos it did not offer daring architectural reconstructions (whether on paper or on the ground), evocative thrones, and colourful frescoes.

Regarding historiographical reasons, the use of prefiguration as a narrative trope might provide an explanation. At least since the 5th BC, the Trojan War has often been portrayed as a prefiguration of the Persian Wars and, later on, of subsequent wars. So, the fall of Knossos could be inserted into this narrative, as a prefiguration of the fall of Troy, and this facilitated a further connection between

---

[31] The use of Aegean and especially Minoan elements in modern reimaginings of the Trojans, albeit puzzling for specialists, are not as surprising as their use in works such as the 1975 film based on Rudyard Kipling's *The Man Who Would Be King*, set in Kafiristan and starring Sean Connery and Michael Caine: here, in addition to Connery's crown, which is based on a Minoan find illustrated by Boucher & Krapf (2014: 196–7), there is a reproduction of the so-called Spring or Swallows fresco from Akrotiri (from 135' 45'''–139''42''' and 146''45'''–149'').

Minoans and Trojans, who were both seen as people defeated and assimilated by the Mycenaeans/Achaeans. This use of prefiguration is exemplified in the novel by Gudmundsson (mentioned earlier) but can also be invoked in the case of Wolfang Petersen's 2004 film *Troy*, albeit through the words of his son, as explained below.

When Petersen was asked in an interview why he had used a mixture of Minoan, Greek, and Near Eastern elements in his *Troy*, he replied in terms of creative licence fostered by the idea that 'nobody knows exactly what the [Trojan] buildings would have looked like' (Winkler, 2015: 19). This response, however, is not entirely satisfactory, since by the time Petersen produced his film there were plenty of reconstructions of Troy that could have been used as models, including reconstructions on display to any visitors to the site since the 1990s. A more interesting explanation was provided by Petersen's son Daniel, who worked as assistant director on the film. His reasons for the use of Minoan elements suggest both aesthetic purposes and the idea of prefiguration:

> the Minoans could not have had any noteworthy contact with Troy in those years . . . the production design corresponds to the authentic history of Troy by using Hittite forms and shapes, *while the echoes of archaic Crete embody a self-contained, purely aesthetic bridge linking the Trojans to the Minoans, who, according to one theory, may themselves have been overrun by the Mycenaeans two hundred years earlier.* (Petersen, 2015: 29, my italics).

4.6 The Emergence of the Cycladic Variant of Aegeomania

The interest in primitivism and exotic arts, which helped the emergence of the Cretomania variant in the first decade of the 20th century, also fuelled other strands of Aegeomania, such as the Cycladic, whose origins can be traced to the first two decades of the 20th century, and especially to the interwar period.

Many archaeologists and art historians have remarked on the affinities between the Cycladic figurines of the 3rd millennium BC (Figure 17) and the works of artists such as Brâncuși, Moore, and Picasso, who enjoyed viewing these Cycladic finds in the Louvre and in the British Museum, made sketches of them, expressed admiration for their simplicity and purity, bought some examples for their own private collections, and produced works of art that were inspired by them or showed great similarities, especially in the 1920s and 1930s (e.g. Renfrew, 1991; Gill & Chippindale, 1993; Renfrew, 2003: 50–8; Chryssovitsanou, 2004 and 2006; Bach, 2006). For example, works by Modigliani and Brancusi that have been compared to Cycladic figurines include the former's *A Woman's Head* (1912), now in the

Figure 17 Henry Moore holding a Cycladic figurine (© David Finn Archive, Department of Image Collections, National Gallery of Art Library, Washington, D. C.).

Metropolitan Museum in New York),[32] and the latter's *Sleeping Muse* (1910), *Torso of a Young Girl* (1922), *The Beginning of the World* (1924) and *Head of a Woman* (1925), although it is uncertain whether these modernist sculptures were influenced by specific Cycladic finds or simply show generic resemblances (Chryssovitsanou, 2004 and 2006, with further references). In other cases, Cycladic influences appear to be better documented: for instance, Chryssovitsanou (2013) reports that Henry Moore's seated figure in alabaster, created in 1930 and now in the Art Gallery of Ontario, was inspired by a photograph of the Cycladic figurine known as 'The Harp Player', and so was Picasso's sculpture *Metamorphoses II*, created in 1928.[33]

---

[32] www.metmuseum.org/art/collection/search/486837.

[33] Moore's seated figure: https://ago.ca/collection/object/76/164; Cycladic 'Harp player': www.namuseum.gr/en/collection/syllogi-kykladikon-archaiotiton/; Picasso's 'Metamorphosis II', www.bridgemanimages.com/en/picasso/metamorphosis-ii-sculpture-by-pablo-picasso-1881-1973-1928-platre-paris-musee-picasso/nomedium/asset/4606311. To the list of artists who owned Cycladic figurines given by Chryssovitsanou (2006), one could add the name of the photographer, art-historian, and art critic Lamberto Vitali (1896–1992): see Pinacoteca di Brera, (2001).

As already suggested, the combined 'Cycladomania' and growing importance of these artists as well as of art critics, such as Christian Zervos,[34]
transformed the Bronze Age Cycladic figurines into *objects d'art*. This, in
turn, affected Aegean archaeology in many ways, including the plundering
and destruction of many Bronze Age sites in the Cyclades to satisfy the
demands of collectors (cf. 1 Introduction and Section 5.4).

4.7 Conclusions

As outlined in this section on Aegeomania and World Wars, the period c. 1915–
45 saw the continuation of some established Aegeomanic trends, such as the use
of Aegean Bronze Age and especially Minoan material culture to illustrate
ancient Greek narratives and stage performances that were set in a distant, pre-
Classical past, thus continuing the processes of familiarization, Hellenization,
and Europeanization of the Aegean Bronze Age that had started in the late 19th
century (cf. Section 2.2). This period also saw the beginning of new trends, such
as the polarization between Minoans and Mycenaeans, and the emergence of
a Cycladic variant of Aegeomania – trends that persisted and even increased in
subsequent decades, with significant repercussions for Aegean archaeology, its
reception, and use in new cultural practices, as discussed below.

5 Aegeomania in a Cold War Environment
(c. Late 1940s–Early 1970s)

5.1 Overview

In the Cold War environment of the late 1940s–early 1970s, which also encom-
passed the growth of second wave feminism and pacifist movements, it is
perhaps not surprising to find that the opposition between Minoans and
Mycenaeans became even more entrenched. This Minoan–Mycenaean dichotomy was often portrayed in specialist and non-specialist works alike in terms of
conflict not only between two powers competing for the same territories, trade
routes, and resources, but also between opposing worldviews, often expressed
in terms of alleged Minoan matriarchy vs Mycenaean patriarchy. The polarization of Minoans and Mycenaeans arguably increased after Michael Ventris'
decipherment of Linear B as Greek in 1952 and the correlated confirmation of
the un-Hellenic character of the language(s) used by the Minoans (as recorded
in the documents written in Linear A and Cretan pictographic/hieroglyphic, and
already suggested by other evidence, e.g. Herodotus I.173). The decipherment

---

[34] See for example Zervos' *L'art en Grèce des temps préhistoriques au début du XVIIIe siècle*
(1934), which contained many illustrations of Cycladic idols. This seminal publication was
followed by his *L'Art des Cyclades* (1957).

of Linear B supported the notion, already well established among many scholars (but not Evans!), that the Mycenaeans, if not exactly identifiable with the Homeric Achaeans, were at least their forefathers. Although for some individuals the Mycenaeans remained hopelessly un-Hellenic (e.g. Martin Heidegger, as discussed below), the notion that Linear B reflected a well-known language and employed common Greek words and names, including those of Olympian deities (e.g. Zeus and Athena), created a new feeling of familiarity. This is illustrated, among other examples, by two poems written by the Nobel laureate Salvatore Quasimodo, after he visited Greece in the 1950s. In his 'Minotauro a Cnossos' (Minotaur at Knossos), Quasimodo depicts Crete as a refined culture, unfettered by the idea of death, but also as rather distant, whereas in his poem on Mycenae there is a feeling of Greekness and Greek affinities, as the poet offers the Lion Gate his Sicilian-Greek greetings:

> Ai Leoni della porta,
> agli scheletri dell'armonia scenica
> rialzati dai filologi delle pietre,
> il mio saluto di siculo greco.

('To the Lions of the gate / to the skeletons of the scenic harmony / re-erected by the philologists of the stones / my Sicilian Greek salute') (Quasimodo, 1958 and 1983).[35]

Besides the further entrenchment of the Minoan–Mycenaean opposition, a significant trend in this period, especially after the Vietnam War, is that pacifism came to be regarded in some quarters as one of the most attractive traits attributable to Minoan Crete, whereas before World War II this was often regarded as a weakness (cf. Section 4.3). This trend was also accompanied by a more critical attitude towards the testimony of the ancient Greek sources and their accounts of the distant Bronze Age past. This, in turn, was partly another consequence of the decipherment of Linear B because, despite the common language and elements of continuity, this had shown some intriguing differences between Mycenaean and Homeric socio-political and economic structures. The critical stance was also partly based on the notions that victors present history as it suits them and that elements of the non-Hellenic Minoan culture may have been lost in translation in the encounter between the two cultures.

Yet, despite a renewed (and growing) appreciation of the Minoans and their alleged pacifism, many Aegeomanic works continue to show a gamut of responses in an ever-increasing variety of genres and cultural practices: whether Minoans, Mycenaeans, Trojans or the inhabitants of the prehistoric Cyclades are paragons of virtue or villains depended not only on general trends but also

---

[35] The poem is also available at www.poesie.reportonline.it/poesie-di-salvatore-quasimodo/poesia-di-salvatore-quasimodo-micene.html

on the individual preferences of writers and artists, who were inspired by their material culture to create something new.

Finally, the most powerful consequences of the Cycladic variant of Aegeomania, which had emerged in the interwar period, came to be felt after World War II with the looting of archaeological sites and the increasing appreciation of Cycladic figurines as artistic treasures.

5.2 Minoan–Mycenaean Dichotomies (and Trojans as Minoans again)

A visual example of Aegeomania that illustrates the entrenchment of the Minoan–Mycenaean opposition in the period after World War II (but before the decipherment of Linear B) appears in the ballet *Minotaur*, which premiered in New York in 1947. This was a modernist retelling of the myth of Theseus and Ariadne, choreographed by John Taras, with music by Elliot Carter, and Aegeanizing costumes by Joan Junyer.[36] The costumes for the Cretan characters were predominantly terracotta, red, tan, and white, whereas yellows and greys were used for the Greeks, specifically to underline the distinction between the two cultures (Junyer, 1947: 164).

After the decipherment of Linear B, among the most famous examples that illustrate the clash between Minoans and Mycenaeans in terms opposite world-views are the historical novel *The King Must Die* (1958) and its sequel *The Bull from the Sea* (1962) by the best-selling author Mary Renault.

Partly inspired by the decipherment of Linear B, the excavations of Grave Circle B at Mycenae by Ioannis Papadimitriou and Giorgos Mylonas (1952–4), and the publication of Robert Graves' *The Greek Myths* (1955), Renault's novels, like many other Aegeomanic works, are modern retellings of Theseus' story, from his childhood in Troizen to his death on the island of Skyros. But they are also, in Renault's own words, a depiction of the 'tensions between victorious patriarchy and lately defeated, still powerful matriarchy' (Renault, 1969: 63).

In Renault's dyad matriarchy appears in a negative light, arguably because the author disapproved of any system in which one gender dominates and individual people are forced to act in stereotypical binary roles, as suggested by her most positive characters – Theseus and his true love, the Amazon Hippolyta – who are rather unconventional in many respects (cf. Sweetman, 1993: 177–8; Zilboorg, 2001: 155–6). Indeed, Renault's Theseus is a luminous hero, while the Minoans or, at least, their elite tend to be presented in ambivalent, darker shades: they are small and often rather effeminate, arrogant, and disdainful of other people, more Oriental than European. Above all, Minoan

---

[36] For some illustrations of Junyer's costumes see www.artic.edu/artists/13269/joan-junyer

society is corrupt and in terminal decline. By the time Theseus visits Knossos, Crete has been under the rule of a strange Graeco-Minoan dynasty for several generations, since Renault follows Evans' dating of the Linear B tablets of Knossos as c. 1400 BC, and takes into account that, according to the Greek tradition, Theseus lived only one generation before the Trojan War (usually dated between c.1250–1180 BC). Renault's hybrid Graeco-Minoan elite follow matrilineal and other Minoan customs to hold on to power, but show no real respect for religion, and mistreat the native Minoans, who are only too ready to follow Theseus' lead and rebel against their detested rulers. Although Renault presents Minoan arts and crafts as bewitching, beneath this beauty there is a heart of darkness, violence, and barbarity. Even Ariadne turns out to be a savage: she takes part in the ritual killing of the king of Dia/Naxos, and this is why a horrified Theseus abandons her. For the Athenian hero Naxos is 'earth-darkness', Crete 'a rotten glow', but Delos (i.e. Greece) is 'lucid, shining, and clear' (Renault, 1958: 256).

Renault (1958: 342–4) makes the fall of the Knossian dynasty partly coincide with the Bronze Age eruption of Santorini/Thera (the date of the final days of Knossos and the volcanic event had not been fully elucidated at that time), but this seems to be largely for dramatic effect. Her explanation for the decline and fall of Minoan Crete almost foreshadows elements of the 'New Archaeology', since her causes are rooted in social processes, which create instability and inability to overcome adversity. In her narrative, there is no recourse to the inevitability of some evolutionary cum-cyclic development from birth to maturity and decline of civilization, nor does she appeal to foreign invasions and natural disasters. The latter may accelerate the outcome, but the ultimate cause of collapse is the rotten political system, the maltreatment of serfs and slaves, which leads to revolt (Renault, 1958: 249; Renault, 1962: 33). Theseus slays King Minos and his stepson (and self-proclaimed successor) Asterion, who is not a monstrous half-bull, half-human creature: the monster in this story is the corrupt and savage regime that Minos and Asterion represent.

Renault's more positive reception of the Mycenaeans/Hellenes is reminiscent of the views expressed by earlier authors in the interwar period and finds an echo in many literary works of the 1950s–60s, which range from novels to travel writing and poetry. An example of this is the *The Maze Maker* (1967) by Michael Ayrton, an intriguing reimagining of the life of Daedalus that is partly an historical novel, and partly a personal, quasi-autobiographical reflection on the life of an artist struggling with his own self. In this work, Daedalus/Ayrton takes a rather dim view of Minoan artists, whom he considers imitative, rigid, and decadent. They only excel in 'an effeminate delicacy of execution', but ... 'their votive bronzes lack all tension; they look as soft or as stringy as

vegetables; nor can the Cretans make large sculpture in wood or stone. ... '
(Ayrton, 2015 [1967]: 77). Above all, their arts 'hang overripe from their minds
or go dry like pomegranates whose skins in time reach the brittleness of fine
Cretan pottery and crack untouched. The gods will burst out through Crete and
spill their red pomegranate seeds on Knossos and Knossos will rot under this
autumn weight' (Ayrton, 2015 [1967]: 77–8). Greece will eventually prevail
over Minoan Crete in artistic ways: in a symbolic scene, Daedalus fights with
a Minotaur, whose face changes during the contest until the monster is transformed
into a marble statue that bears 'no longer the stupid and yet familiar countenance of
a bull but that of a kouros carved from marble' (Ayrton, 2015 [1967]: 200).

Another work illustrating a preference for things Greek over Minoan Crete is
Viaggio nella Grecia Antica (1954), a travelogue by Cesare Brandi, an influential art historian and leading scholar in the field of conservation–restoration
theory, who became the first director of the Istituto Centrale del Restauro in
Rome. He abhorred Evans' restorations and thought that they made the famous
throne of Knossos look 'pretentious and ridiculous' (Brandi, 2006 [1954]: 27–
8). Although Brandi found other Minoan sites and some finds in the Heraklion
Museum interesting, his overall conclusion was that the Minoans had not really
produced something that could be called 'art' and, besides, must have been
a rather peculiar people, because they tightly swaddled infants' waists (to
produce figures with wasp-waists), cruelly forced women to bare their breasts,
and could not be a matriarchy, despite some notable feminine traits in their
iconography (Brandi, 2006 [1954]: 30–3, 42–3). If Brandi found Minoan Crete,
and especially Knossos, rather disappointing, by contrast his visit to Mycenae
was highly rewarding. He appreciated the unadorned barbaric grandiosity of the
Mycenaean ruins and found magnificence, and even magic, in the roughly hewn
blocks of the citadel's walls, in the Lion Gate, and in the Shaft Grave circle
excavated by Schliemann (Brandi, 2006 [1954]: 95–8).

An antipathy for things Minoan is further illustrated in a later travelogue by the
German philosopher Martin Heidegger, who visited Greece in 1962 (Heidegger,
2005). His reaction to the site of Knossos and the Minoan finds in the Heraklion
Museum was that they represented an Oriental world, an interesting, shiny
civilisation, but also superficial, and so unattractive to him that he preferred to
stay on his boat rather than pay a visit to Phaistos (Heidegger, 2005: 22–4). Unlike
Brandi, however, Heidegger was not impressed by the Mycenaean world either,
because he felt that it was not Greek enough: 'We were about to visit Mycenae.
I felt a resistance against the pre-Hellenic world [sic], although it was the critical
exchange with it that first helped the Greeks to grasp their proper element'
(Heidegger, 2005: 22). His resistance was so strong that he did not report
a single impression about his visit to the citadel of the Atreids.

In the 1950s–early 1970s, however, other authors felt more enthused by the Minoans than the Mycenaeans, precisely because of their otherness, alleged pacifism, and other reasons. For instance, the French author Jacques Lacarrière, who visited Greece in the 1950s, was enchanted by Minoan Crete, which for him had a taste of lost paradise, whereas he found Mycenae oppressive (Lacarrière, 1975: 119–45 for visit to Crete; 175–82, for visit to Mycenae). When visiting Knossos and the Heraklion Museum, unencumbered by any historical or literary baggage, he felt as if he was leafing through a book, which offered something attractive and unusual on every page, intriguingly different from Greece and so unlike what transpired in later Greek mythology. According to Lacarrière, the ruins of Knossos emanated a sense of freedom and osmosis between palace and town; those of Mycenae evoked oppression and isolation. In addition, for Lacarrière Minoan Crete, and especially the site of Phaistos, felt feminine and full of joy, whereas Mycenae felt steeped in death and matricide, as if the Greeks needed to kill the mother (the *genos*) to create the brotherhood of the *polis* – something vaguely reminiscent of the alleged struggle between matriarchy and patriarchy in Renault's novels and in many other earlier and later works.

Renault's novels portrayed Theseus as a hero, but her views were not shared by other authors, such as Roger Lancelyn Green, an authority on children's literature, who also wrote and edited many children's books. In his *Mystery at Mycenae* (1957), Green effectively equates Mycenaeans and Achaeans, and presents Theseus as a great villain: not only was his record with women (from Helen to Phaedra) appalling, but he was a usurper (Menestheus being portrayed as the rightful king of Athens), and a murderer to boot. Green's text and the illustrations by Margery Gill show some traces of Aegeomania, but rather faint, since the allusions to the material culture of the Aegean Bronze Age are minimal (e.g. the Vaphio cup, the Lion Gate). Author and illustrator also take many archaeological liberties: for example, there are mentions of marble floors, marble baths, large statues, and other Classical anachronisms; moreover, some walls appear to be decorated with tapestries, instead of frescoes, as one would expect in Mycenaean palaces, and women are dressed in a classicizing manner, not as one finds in Aegean Bronze Age iconography, although this could be explained by the need to avoid showing bare breasts to young readers.

Green's slightly later *The Luck of Troy* (1961), also illustrated by Gill, presents some Achaean characters in a negative light once again (e.g. Palamedes as a traitor) but also shows a closer engagement with and attention to archaeological niceties, albeit almost exclusively when referring to Mycenae, where part of the action takes place. For example, in addition to the famous Lion Gate, Treasury of Atreus, the Shaft Grave circle excavated by Schliemann, and other architectural features, Green mentions an object made of rock crystal shaped like a duck, which is a reference to an exquisite find from grave omicron in Shaft Graves Circle B (excavated in the 1950s),[37] and reports a message written in Linear B on a clay tablet (Green, 1961: 9–19 and 106–7). By contrast, when it comes to Troy, the archaeological details are few and far between, and not very Trojan. Even in the chapter titled 'Polyxena's bracelet' there is no real description of her bracelet and other jewellery, which is surprising, since some of Schliemann's famous Trojan finds (e.g. 'Priam's treasure' and 'Helen's jewels') could have provided obvious models.

If Renault's novels showed a marked preference for the Mycenaean/Achaean Greeks and Green's children stories cast doubts about the virtues of some Achaean/Mycenaean characters, other Aegeomanic works of this period present them in a decidedly negative light and show more sympathy for both Trojans and Minoans. For example, in the film *Helen of Troy* (1956) directed by Robert Wise, the Achaeans are sleazy warmongers: they were already planning to destroy Troy well before Paris' fateful encounter with Helen, whereas the Trojans are a peace-seeking folk; perhaps it is no coincidence that Wise's Troy looks like a Minoan palace (Figure 18).

A less than enchanted view of warlike Mycenaeans and a rehabilitation of the peaceful Minoans also appear in two rather different literary works of this period: Thomas Burnett Swann's fantasy trilogy – *Day of the Minotaur* (1966), *The Forest*

Figure 18 Screenshot from *Helen of Troy* (1956) directed by
Robert Wise, showing Minoan architectural features (e.g. columns, 'horns of consecration').

---

[37] See www.namuseum.gr/en/collection/syllogi-mykinaikon-archaiotiton/

Forever (1971), and *Cry Silver Bells* (published posthumously in 1977) – and the science fiction novel *The Dancer from Atlantis* (1971) by the prolific author Poul Anderson.

Day of the Minotaur is another Aegeomanic work that nicely shows the impact of the decipherment of Linear B. It starts jokily with a preface in which the author claims that this book will compensate for the disappointment caused among scholars by the discovery that the Linear B tablets are mere palatial inventories, since here he publishes the contents of a papyrus discovered on Crete, which contains a proper historical account of events that took place 'soon after 1500 B.C.', namely the victorious alliance of 'Beasts' and Minoans against one of the many Mycenaean/Achaean attacks on Crete that had increased after the eruption of Santorini/Thera (Swann, 1966: 5–6).

In all three novels by Swann the Minoans are portrayed according to well-established characterizations: they are a civilized, peaceful, trading nation, fighting only against pirates or invaders, unlike the warlike and rather uncouth Achaeans/Mycenaeans; moreover, the Minoans are sexually liberated, their women have considerable power, and they worship a Great Mother Goddess, whose cult rituals include bull leaping, drugs, and ecstatic dancing. If these are all traits that appear in previous works by specialists and non-specialists alike (including many Aegeomanic novels), there is one element in Swann's depiction of the Minoans that is rather unusual, namely his idea of their relationship with the natural world. According to Swann, the Minoans fear nature 'unless they can put her in chains' (Swann, 1966: 116), and this disagrees with their more traditional conception as a people worshipping, empathizing, and living in harmony with the natural world (see e.g. Hawkes, 1968 and 1980; Shapland, 2022: 11). Yet Swann's view seems to anticipate the less idealistic, but more discerning, interpretation recently offered by Andrew Shapland (2022: 16), who has argued that the 'naturalistic' iconography of Minoan Crete has more to do with claims of territorial and animal domination by the Knossian elite, 'whose expansion was undoubtedly accompanied by violence against humans and non-humans'.

In the Cold War period, another positive depiction of Minoan Crete appears in Anderson's *The Dancer from Atlantis* (1971). Like Renault's novels and many other works, this is partly a retelling of the myth of Theseus and the Minotaur, interpreted as a folk memory of the fall of the Minoans at the hand of conquering Achaeans–Mycenaeans. Anderson (1971: 70–1), however, explicitly takes issue with Renault (and Classical sources). He offers an unsympathetic account of Theseus and a glowing portrait of Minoan Crete even if, in the end, he concedes that Theseus and the Greeks are not entirely a bad lot, if only because they are the inheritors of Minoan culture. The novel makes a nod to emerging second wave feminism and anticipates the even more radically anti-patriarchal reimaginings of Greek mythology in some Aegeomanic novels published in subsequent decades.

Similarly, *The Last Heracles* (1971) by Georgia Sallaska (one of the pseudonyms used by American author Georgia Myrle Miller) presents the Mycenaeans in a relatively positive light, but only because they have been influenced by Minoan culture, especially when it comes to their relationship with women. This novel is a modern retelling of the story of Heracles and his famous twelve labours, but it is set a generation or two after the Trojan war, at the time of the mythical invasion by the Dorians, who are portrayed as evil, barbaric, and patriarchal. In Sallaska's version, Heracles appears as 'a sacred king, nominally the son of a god, pledged to a goddess, and working with a twin', whose original character was distorted in later Greek myths because the 'late-coming patriarchal invaders ... usurped the hero for his attractive qualities and made him their own' (Sallaska, 1974 [1971]: 14). The last Mycenaeans, including the last Heracles, are still relatively Minoanized and therefore civilized: for example, they use the fist to forehead salute that one finds in Minoan iconography, their elite women and priestesses wear the typical 'Minoan' dress with open bodice, they have kings but they pay respect to goddesses, and still have memories of the old matriarchal regime. As Sallaska recounts, during the Trojan War 'women had taken the power back into their hands as it had been in the old days before the Sons of Ion and the Sons of Aeolus had come' (Sallaska, 1974 [1971]: 53). By contrast, the Dorians are 'barbarians who know only how to rape, and kill, and destroy' (Sallaska, 1974 [1971]: 49), and 'women were only a little better than cattle to them; the worship of a goddess was beyond their comprehension' (Sallaska, 1974 [1971]: 61). Besides the archaeological touches mentioned above, the novel contains references to frescoes and to Linear B. Indeed, according to Sallaska (1974 [1971]: 211), the Linear B tablets found at Pylos reveal that Nestor was so excessively obsessed with bureaucracy that the Messenians got tired of him – an intriguing alternative explanation of the fall of Pylos, which might resonate with many people whose lives are blighted by too much paperwork.

5.3 Linear B Beyond Literary Works

The decipherment of Linear B had an impact well beyond literary works, and some intriguing examples are attested in the visual arts, such as the surprising inclusion of Linear B in one of the stained-glass lancet windows that decorate the All Saints chapel of the University of the South, Sewanee, in the US State of Tennessee.

This window was created by Arthur Frederick Erridge of J. Wippell & Co. in Exeter (UK) in the late 1950s and may have been designed under the instructions of a Professor of Classics in Sewanee, Bayly Turington (Palaima & McDonough, 2016). The lancet windows of this chapel meant to represent the various departments in Sewanee at the time, and the one connected with Classics depicts the figure of St Clement of Alexandria, surrounded by Greek emblems and inscriptions taken from texts by Plato and St Clement, besides Linear B. The latter is represented by an inscribed stirrup jar from Tiryns and a tablet from Knossos. As argued by Palaima and McDonough (2016: 237), this work conveys the idea of the long continuum of 'western knowledge about the nature of human beings in the world and in relation to the divine sphere from the earliest readable written texts' (Linear B) to St Clement, who forms 'the bridge [from antiquity] to Christian writings'.

Less surprising are the uses of Linear B (and other Aegean scripts) in the works of other visual artists (and writers) of the mid 20th century, who shared a deep interest in signs and symbols and, more generally, were fascinated by the connection between art and writing, as illustrated by the popularity in this period of Visual or Concrete Poetry (a.k.a. Skripturale Malerei: see e.g. Bann, 1967).

Examples of this interest in signs and symbols are paintings by the Italian artists Antonino Nacci and Gastone Novelli (La Rosa & Militello, 2006: 251). In the early 1960s, Novelli visited Greece and sketched some Linear B signs (Figure 19; see also Novelli, 1966), and Linear B signs can later be found in his

Figure 19 Gastone Novelli, *Viaggio in Grecia (Lineare B)* (1961–3), pencil on cardboard, 50x35 cm (photo Courtesy Archivio Gastone Novelli).

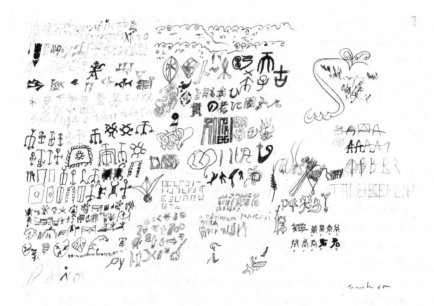

Figure 20 Gastone Novelli, *Tavola Degli Ornamenti* (1965), pencil and pen on paper, 49x71 cm (photo Courtesy Archivio Gastone Novelli).

1965 work 'Tavola degli ornamenti' (table of the ornaments) (Figure 20), together with signs from many other types of writing, such as Egyptian Hieroglyphic, the Greek alphabet, Cuneiform, and the Phaistos Disk. Novelli was also fascinated by the links between writing, magic, and alchemy, and it is no coincidence that a version of the mysterious Phaistos Disk was used for the cover of a collection of his essays, published posthumously in 2019 (Novelli, 2019).

5.4 Cycladomania in the Cold War (and Beyond)

As indicated above, the Cycladic variant of Aegeomania that emerged in the interwar period had powerful consequences in subsequent decades. In fact, one can debate the significance and extent of Cycladic influence on famous modern artists, but there can be little doubt that these artists' growing reputation, especially after World War II, transformed the perception of Cycladic finds, especially marble figurines, as *objets d'art* because of the perceived similarities between these ancient objects and their artworks. The elevation of Cycladic objects, especially figurines, to the status of high art, was shared by collectors and archaeologists alike in the first decades of the Cold War, as shown by publications and exhibitions in archaeological museums (see e.g. Thimme,1977; Getz-Preziosi, 1987, with earlier references) and culminated in the creation in 1986 of the Museum of Cycladic Art in Athens. This perception of Cycladic objects, in turn, created a demand for them among collectors, and the need to satisfy this demand resulted in the looting and destruction of many Bronze Age sites in the Aegean, in thefts from museums, and in the creation of forgeries (see e.g. Renfrew, 1991: 28; Gill & Chippindale, 1993: 603, 610, 616, 624).

Nowadays the looting has somewhat abated, partly because, over the years, more and more countries have ratified the 1970 UNESCO convention on the illicit trafficking of cultural property, making it more difficult for looters to dispose of their booty,[38] but also because there is not much left to loot, especially in terms of Cycladic Bronze Age cemeteries (Gill & Chippindale, 1993: 610 and 625). The appreciation of Cycladic objects as high art, however continues to the present day, as indicated, for example, by the word 'treasure' in the very title of an exhibition that opened in the Museum of Cycladic Art on 3 November 2022: 'Homecoming: Cycladic treasures on a return voyage'.[39] In fact, one should not forget that this museum opened to display the private collection of antiquities of Dolly and Nikolaos Goulandris, which includes a considerable number of Cycladic figurines of dubious provenance, described on the museum website as captivating 'the visitor with their simplicity and abstractness, elements that have inspired some of the 20th-century's greatest artists, such as Konstantin Brancusi, Amedeo Modigliani, Alberto Giacometti, Barbara Hepworth, and Henry Moore'.[40]

One wonders, however, whether these figurines would have been so admired had they preserved the lurid colours that originally adorned their surfaces, or had these colours been indicated on reconstructive drawings and on all the replicas on sales in many Greek museums (on the pigments that decorated the figurines see e.g. Hendrix, 2003; Birtacha, 2016). It is possible that some of the modern artists mentioned above would have found their bright decorations rather attractive, as evocative of 'primitive' art, but it is more difficult to see how they might have sustained their admiration for their purity and simplicity. Also, would brightly painted figurines have inspired the intriguing poem 'Cycladic Idols' by David Constantine, published in his 1998 collection *The Pelt of Wasps*, whose cover illustrates a Cycladic figurine?

In any case, even if some viewers (including Constantine) are perfectly aware that the figurines were originally brightly coloured, they are now white, and their whiteness not only evokes simplicity and purity, but can also be linked to

---

[38] https://en.unesco.org/fighttrafficking/1970

[39] https://cycladic.gr/en/page/girismos-kikladiki-thisauri-sto-taxidi-tis-epistrofis. The Metropolitan Museum in New York also hosted an exhibition on Cycladic art from a private collection in 2024 (www.metmuseum.org/exhibitions/cycladic-art).

[40] https://cycladic.gr/en/page/about-us.

common visualization of Classical Greek sculptures and enduring Winckelmannian ideas of Greece. Classical Greek sculptures were also brightly coloured, but have been perceived, appreciated, and idealized as white, especially since the publication of Winckelmann's influential *Geschichte der Kunst des Alterthums* (1764), which highlighted whiteness and purity, despite showing awareness of ancient polychromy (see e.g. Brinkmann, 2017; Hodne, 2022).

The idealization of whiteness in both Cycladic and later Greek sculpture unfortunately dies hard and found a spectacular illustration in the opening ceremony of the Athens Olympics in 2004.[41] In the very opening scenes the gigantic white head of a Cycladic figurine emerges from the sea: after geometric and mathematical symbols are projected onto it, it bursts into fragments and, from inside it, the statue of an Archaic kouros emerges (also shown as white); this, in turn, breaks into fragments, and the statue of a Classical kouros appears (again, also all white); this also becomes fragmented, and the scene eventually gives way to the 'Clepsydra', a parade of tableaux representing important eras of Greek history, which starts with the Minoans and ends in the late 19th century, with the reinvention of the Olympic games, but significantly overlooks the Roman and Ottoman periods of Greek history.[42] Even a decade later, in 2015, the Chinese artist Ai Weiwei produced a completely white, life-size marble sculpture inspired by the ancient Cycladic figurines for his 2016 exhibition in the Museum of Cycladic Art ('Standing Figure', 2015).[43] His use of marble is a homage to Greece, but given that this exhibition was also a vehicle to highlight the refugees' crisis in the Mediterranean, many of whom are not white or do not necessarily identify with the Winckelmannian ideas of beauty and purity, one wonders whether the use of a marble statue with bright colours would have been more provocative and subversive as well as more historically/archaeologically accurate.

5.5 Conclusions

Alongside the continuation of trends already present in the interwar period (such as the polarization between Minoans and Mycenaeans, and the Cycladic variant of Aegeomania), during the Cold War era the alleged Minoan pacifism

---

[41] See e.g. www.youtube.com/watch?v=YYvnvr8Cpzo

[42] The 'Clepsydra' of the 2004 Athens Olympics may be seen as the culmination of earlier parades illustrating the exclusion of Romans and Ottomans and the curious incorporation of the non-Hellenic Minoans into the long continuum of Greek history. Examples of these, among others, are the parades created by the Lyceum of Greek Women in the 1920s to celebrate the centenary of the Greek War of Independence (Momigliano, 2020: 129, with further references). For an illustration of the Minoan costumes created for one of these pageants see Florou (2016).

[43] https://cycladic.gr/en/page/ai-weiwei-at-cycladic

came to be seen in a more positive light – and Minoan Crete became a kind of lost paradise, largely forgotten until archaeologists rediscovered it. In addition, the strong fascination with the testimony of the ancient Greek sources, from Homer to Plutarch, and their relationship with Aegean Bronze Age realities continued, and so did the conviction that these sources contained a kernel of historical truth. In fact, in many Aegeomanic works (and not only of the Cold War period) Aegean Bronze Age material culture is used simply to provide some local colour to modern retellings of some famous ancient Greek myths. In other cases, however, one can see an attempt to use Aegean Bronze Age archaeology to present different versions of these old stories, and for the period treated in this Section 5, especially after the decipherment of Linear B, one can even detect a growing appreciation of the disjuncture and incongruity between later Greek sources and Bronze Age realities. This trend appears to foreshadow later Aegeomanic works, which are even more drastic reimaginings of traditional ancient Greek narratives, show a stronger focus on material culture and Linear B, or even ignore the ancient Greek sources entirely, as discussed in the following Section 6, on Post-Modern Aegeomania.

6 Post-Modern Aegeomania (c. Mid 1970s–Late 1990s)

6.1 Overview

The period from the mid 1970s till the end of the 20th century, encompassing the end of the Vietnam War, the collapse of the Soviet Union, and the end of the Cold War, witnessed intriguing shifts in the reception and uses of the Aegean Bronze Age in both specialist and non-specialist works. The materialist attitudes of the Thatcher–Reagan era, the critical post-modern frames of mind, and the discoveries in the summer of 1979 of possible human sacrifice as well as ritual cannibalism at Anemospilia-Archanes and at Knossos, all helped to undermine the idealized image of Minoan Crete as a lost paradise of peaceful, sexually liberated, very civilized, and egalitarian people, which had become even more popular since World War II (for archaeological discoveries see Sakellarakis & Sapouna-Sakellaraki, 1981; Warren, 1981a, 1981b; Wall *et al.*, 1986; Sakellarakis & Sakellarakis, 1997: 268–311).

Yet, if the Minoans lost lustre and (re)acquired a dark side in some Aegeomanic works of this period, in others one finds some of the most idealized representations of Minoan Crete as a gender-egalitarian paradise and, conversely, some of the most violent and bloodthirsty depictions of the Mycenaeans/Achaeans. This is largely because the growth of second wave feminism and the Goddess Movement prompted a search for alternative, female-voiced narratives and feminist icons: the already well-established Minoan–Mycenaean dichotomy provided a ready-made canvas upon which new myths could be painted. In addition, the spectacular discoveries made at the Cycladic settlement of Akrotiri on Thera/Santorini, the Pompeii of the Aegean, continue to be alluded to in many Aegeomanic novels, since the eruption of the Thera/Santorini volcano is implicated in the decline and fall of the Minoans and rise of the Mycenaeans – arguably the most common topic in Aegeomanic literature. Beyond literature, among the most graceful Aegeomanic works of this period are some garments from the 1994 spring–summer collection created by the renowned couturier Karl Lagerfeld for the Parisian fashion house Chloé, which were largely inspired by the frescoes from Akrotiri.

6.2 Beneath the Minoan Lilies and Blue Monkeys: the Dark Side of the Minoans and Post-Modern Introspections

Intriguing explorations of the dark side of Minoan Crete and the use of Aegean Bronze age material culture as a catalyst for introspective reflexions appear in the novel *The Names* (1982) and the short story 'The Ivory Acrobat' (1988) by the American writer Don DeLillo.[44]

In *The Names*, two of the characters engage in a dialogue that ironically and skilfully mentions some of the most common clichés about the Minoans (their sophistication, gracefulness, love of colour and nature, and *joie de vivre*) but also hints at 'Darker things. Beneath the lilies and antelopes and blue monkeys' – darker things that are suggested by the later Greek legends of the Minotaur and his labyrinth and, above all, by the excavations at Anemospilia-Archanes that 'turned up signs of human sacrifice' (DeLillo, 1982: 84). Instead of being upset by this revelation about the dark side of the Minoans, one of the characters feels gratification, because this concurs with his tendency to expect the worst: 'Satisfaction … always the self finds a place for its fulfilments, even in the Cretan wild, outside time and light' (DeLillo, 1982: 85).[45]

In addition, DeLillo's reflections on Aegean Bronze Age objects, their materiality, agency, entanglements with humans, and relationship to selfhood curiously intersect and contrast with relatively recent debates on the 'material turn' and even the 'sensory turn' in many fields, including Minoan archaeology.[46] Thus, one of the characters in *The Names*, while reflecting on some excavations on an

---

[44] The short story was originally published in *Granta* 12, Autumn 1988: https://granta.com/the-ivory-acrobat/.

[45] *The Names* also describes some fictional recent ritual killings that had occurred in Greece as a modern version of the Minoan human sacrifice of Anemospilia-Archanes as a 'latter-day plea to the gods', while recalling that some Linear B tablets seem to list human offerings (DeLillo, 1982: 116).

[46] On the 'material turn' and 'material-culture turn' see e.g. Latour (2005); Miller (2005); Ingold (2007); Bennett & Joyce (2010); Hicks (2010); Hodder (2012). On the 'sensory turn', see e.g. Howes (2006, 2013, 2018) and, in a Minoan context, Hamilakis (2013).

Aegean island, remarks that 'Maybe objects are consoling. Old ones in particular, earth-textured, made by other-minded men. Objects are what we aren't, what we can't extend ourselves to be. Do people make things to define the boundaries of the self? Objects are the limits we desperately need. They show us where we end. They dispel our sadness, temporarily' (DeLillo, 1982: 133).

These ideas are further elaborated in relationship to a specific Minoan object in DeLillo's short story 'The Ivory Acrobat', which takes its title after a well-known ivory figurine of a bull-leaper from Knossos, on display in the Heraklion Museum.[47] DeLillo's short story recounts how Kyle, a young American school-teacher, experienced an earthquake in Athens during the early 1980s. The tremors had caused the breakage of one of her possessions, a terracotta head of Hermes, and so her friend Edmund gives her a replica of a Minoan bull-leaper to replace it. This replica, however, unlike the Minoan original, represents a female bull-leaper, which is an allusion to the popular idea that both male and female youths performed this dangerous activity (although this is now rejected by most scholars, who believe all bull-leapers to be male: see Shapland, 2013, with further bibliography).[48] For Edmund the replica recalls Kyle's 'hidden litheness', the fact that she is 'lean and supple and young . . . throbbing with inner life' (DeLillo, 2011 [1988]: 66–7). But Kyle does not see the connection: for her, the figurine is something strange, distant, and mysteri-ous, unlike the 'knowable past' represented by the Hermes head. Yet, the gracefulness, tactility, and materiality as well as the otherness of the Minoan replica are a catalyst for Kyle's self-awareness, for defining her selfhood, and she ends up carrying it with her everywhere, like a talisman. In DeLillo's words:

> Edmund had said the figure was like her. She studied it, trying to extract the sparest recognition. A girl in a loincloth and wristband, double-necklaced, suspended over the horns of a running bull. The act, the leap itself, might be vaudeville or sacred terror. There were themes and secrets and storied lore in this six-inch figure that Kyle could not begin to guess at. She turned the object in her hand. All the facile parallels fell away. Lithe, young, buoyant, modern; rumbling bulls and quaking earth. There was nothing that might connect her to the mind inside the work, an ivory carver, 1600 BC, moved by forces remote from her. She remembered the old earthen Hermes, flower-crowned, looking out at her from a knowable past, some shared theater of being. The Minoans were outside all this. Narrow-waisted, graceful, other-minded – lost across vales of language and magic, across dream cosmologies. This was the

---

[47] www.heraklionmuseum.gr/en/collections/

[48] The idea that in Minoan Crete both female and male youths took part in the bull-leaping activities (with the women dressed as men) goes back to Evans (1901: 94; 1935: 28), and this idea dies hard – it continues to appear also in some museums' websites (see e.g. www.penn.museum/sites/expedition/bulls-and-bull-leaping-in-the-minoan-world/)

piece's little mystery. It was a thing in opposition, defining what she was not, marking the limits of the self. She closed her fist around it firmly and thought she could feel it beat against her skin with a soft and periodic pulse, an earthliness . . . Her self-awareness ended where the acrobat began. Once she realized this, she put the object in her pocket and took it everywhere (DeLillo, 2011 [1988]: 72).

Minoan material culture as a catalyst for self-exploration also looms large in the novel *Prince of the Lilies* (1991) by the Australian writer Rod Jones, which illustrates not only the fall from grace of the Minoans but also aspects of the history of archaeology, in a Minoan context, from the romantic and culture-history approach of Evans to more recent processual and post-processual approaches, and even anticipates, albeit unwittingly and to a limited extent, the sensory turn of the discipline.[49] To an Aegean Bronze Age scholar, this novel reads almost like the fictional counterpart of an essay by the archaeologist Sheena Crawford (1983), in which she criticized both early approaches to Minoan archaeology as 'thinly-disguised libidinal fantasies of repressed athletes and nature-lovers', and more modern approaches as equally 'unsatisfactory precisely because of their complete rejection of all that is lyrical in favour of the coldly compartmentalized, separatist outlook'; besides, Crawford candidly remarked that she gave up aspects of her research because she found it impossible effectively to combine new approaches and methodologies with the available data (Crawford, 1983: 47).[50] In Jones' novel, the main character, the archaeologist Charles Saracen, maintains that 'in one sense the entire enterprise of Minoan archaeology was a kind of libidinal fantasy' and gives up his project on the Minoan Golden Age, after becoming disillusioned with Evans' 'sunny view of the Minoans' (Jones, 1991: 58) and with his own scholarly but pedantic methodology. As other archaeologists bring to light evidence of Minoan ritual cannibalism and human sacrifice, he becomes more interested in a sensory and sensuous approach to the Minoan past.[51]

Jones' *Prince of the Lilies* was 'the inspirational trigger' for the 1996 poetry volume *Crete* by a fellow Australian writer, Dorothy Porter, which includes over forty poems inspired by the island's Minoan past (Porter, 1996: ix). In these poems Minoan Crete emerges as a paradoxical island, at the same time luminous and dark, enchanting and terrifying. For example, in 'The Laws of Volcanoes' and 'The Power and the Glory' Crete is mysterious, sensuous, wondrous, 'volatilely feminine',

---

[49] On the sensory turn cf. p. 48 and note 46; for processual and post-processual turns in archaeology see e.g. Trigger (2006).

[50] Jones (1991: 175–6) openly acknowledges the influence of papers such as those published by Crawford (1983) and Bintliff (1984), among others.

[51] An interesting novel that also shows the dark side of the Minoans while tracing the history of Minoan studies, from romantic Evans to processual archaeology, is Roderick Beaton's *Ariadne's Children* (1995).

a place where 'the breast' appears to have been 'mightier than the sword', while in 'The beautiful friend' and 'Blue Monkey Flying Through an Orchard', Porter affirms that 'nothing is more passionate than a Minoan octopus' and the blue monkeys are 'lighter than life'. At the same time, the brilliant images evoked by Minoan archaeology in her poetry are juxtaposed to others that are drenched in blood, terror, and violence. Thus, for instance, the poems 'Exuberance with bloody hands', 'Atlantis', 'The Body', 'Lost Civilisation', and 'Triumph of the Will' allude to human sacrifice, cannibalism, and bull-leaping as a dangerous blood-lusty spectacle. In 'Atlantis', in particular, the Minoans are compared to Lithuanians, who clapped every time the victim of a pogrom was beaten to death, and even to the Nazis: despite all the Minoan wonders, not all was 'glorious among the slithering lilies'.

As a final example of Aegeomanic works of the last quarter of the 20th century, which offer an ambiguous take on the Minoans, I would like to mention the science-fiction franchise *Stargate*. In the episode 'The Broca Divide',[52] in the first Stargate television series (broadcast in 1997), the SG1 team (the flagship team of the Stargate Command) heads for planet P3X-797, which is divided into two opposite sides: one is the Land of Light, inhabited by civilized people who live in what looks like a Minoan palace (Figures 21–22) and are descendants of the Minoans; the other is

Figure 21 *Stargate* TV series: screenshot of 'The Broca Divide' episode (1997): a view of the palace of the people of the Land of Light.

---

[52] The title of the episode refers to Paul Broca (1824-80), a French surgeon, neurologist and physical anthropologist, who wrote many articles on brain anatomy. A region of the frontal lobe that is responsible for articulated language is named after him, and is mentioned by one of the Stargate characters, Dr Daniel Jackson, after visiting the Land of the Dark (https://stargate .fandom.com/wiki/The_Broca_Divide).

Figure 22 *Stargate* TV series: screenshot of 'The Broca Divide' episode (1997): entrance to the palace of the people of the Land of Light.

the Land of Dark, which is inhabited by banished citizens of the Land of Light, who have contracted a mysterious disease that leads them to savagery and live in a dark forest.[53] Liz Bourke (2014:13) has suggested that, despite the numerous allusions to the material culture of Bronze Age Crete, rather than the Minoans, this episode represents 'a very Classical division of the intellect and the passions: between self-control and self-forgetfulness, between *eunomia*, good order, and disorder'; in other words, Star Gate's Minoans, 'In their role as a kind of metaphor-made-flesh … recall to our attention that perhaps some of the attraction Evans' Minoan civilization holds for the modern age is because of all the things we do not know, the things we cannot know about Cretan life in the Bronze Age'. This perceptive suggestion, however, does not exclude the idea that this episode also alludes to views of the Minoans resurfacing in this period, according to which Minoan Crete was not an unqualified paradise, but a place that was civilized and barbarous at the same time, as illustrated by examples of Aegeomanic novels and poetry discussed above.

6.3 Minoan Heroines, Mycenaean Murderers: Minoan Paradise Regained?

In his aptly titled essay, 'Happy little extroverts and bloodthirsty tyrants: Minoans and Mycenaeans in literature in English after Evans and Schliemann', David Roessel (2006: 205) writes:

---

[53] www.imdb.com/title/tt0709181/; www.dailymotion.com/video/x5vfzsv. There are also references to Linear A in the 'Brief Candle' episode: see www.gateworld.net/sg1/s1/brief-candle/transcript/.

there are contemporary reasons for why Schliemann's Mycenaeans were imagined as warriors and Evans' Minoans as pacifists. But there is something attractive in the perceived juxtaposition of the two cultures, which has served to distort the popular impression of both. If the Minoans are to mean something different in the future, if they are to seem less idealised, then the Mycenaeans may have to become more human. But even then, we will continue to use both the Minoans and the Mycenaeans for our own purposes.

As discussed in the previous section, less idealized Minoans appear in some works of the mid 1970s–late1990s, but this was not because the Mycenaeans became 'more human'. On the contrary, in some works of this period they seem to have become even more brutal and bloodthirsty. This is especially clear in some Aegeomanic novels, which were influenced by second and third wave feminism, especially by the work of Lithuanian-American archaeologist Marija Gimbutas. She revived and popularized the old idea that patriarchy replaced matriarchy in the Bronze Age thanks to her 'Kurgan hypothesis', according to which hordes of patriarchal Indo-Europeans originating from the Pontic steppes vanquished the largely peaceful, matriarchal societies that had emerged in Neolithic Eurasia (Gimbutas, 1974 and 1982; Gimbutas & Dexter, 1999). In this scenario, Minoan Crete represented one of the last matriarchal bastions against Indo-European expansion, until the island succumbed to Mycenaean rulers in the mid 2nd millennium BC.

The Aegeomanic novels influenced by Gimbutas foreground female voices to present alternative narratives that do not glorify male power and war, but cast light on the realities of violence, rape, and murder. Typical examples are some modern reimaginings of the myth of Theseus, in which female characters take central stage, such as June Rachuy Brindel's novels *Ariadne* (1980) and *Phaedra* (1985). Like the earlier historical novels by Renault discussed above, Brindel's dyad is rich in archaeological details, considers the myth of Theseus as a metaphor for the (patriarchal) Mycenaean takeover of (matri-archal) Minoan Crete, and seems to suggest that no system in which one gender predominates is a good thing. Brindel's Minoan Crete, however, is cast in a sympathetic light, whereas Theseus is a rather flawed hero – a brute who becomes obsessed with power and with suppressing the cult of the Mother Goddess to replace it with his patriarchal Olympian religion. In Brindel's new version of the myth, to accomplish his goal Theseus exterminates scores of women, especially priestesses of the Mother Goddess cult, including his own mother and a daughter from his marriage to Phaedra, because the little girl represented the last goddess on earth of the old matriarchal religion; he also kills his son Hippolytus because he truly loves Phaedra, abhors violence, and believes in the old religion.

Another work that offers a rather dim view of the Mycenaeans (and a flattering one of the Minoans) is Judith Hand's historical novel *Voice of the Goddess*. This, like Brindel's dyad, is also partly inspired by Gimbutas and alludes to the material culture of the Aegean Bronze Age (especially of Knossos) but does not take its cue from the myth of Theseus. Instead, the main inspiration is the eruption of Thera and its consequences. The novel focuses on the struggle between two religious factions (representing matriarchy and patriarchy): one supports peace and harmony and is devoted to the traditional cult of the Mother Goddess; the other worships a male, earth-shaker god, and is supported by Mycenaeans and by Cretans who have come under their sway.[54] Crete is imagined as a deeply religious, peaceful, advanced, and egalitarian society, ruled by a High Priestess guided by a council of elderly women. Minoan men may not hold the highest offices, but they are the 'finest lovers in the world' (Hand, 2001 [1999]: 107). This idyllic picture is only marginally spoilt by Hand's suggestion that the Minoans disapprove of mixed-race marriages and show bigoted adherence to religious rituals and other traditions. Overall, however, Hand's Minoans are a model society, 'elegant and peaceful' and 'a source of great hope for humanity' (Hand, 2001[1999]: 376). The Mycenaeans/Achaeans, on the other hand, are a rather bad lot – bloodthirsty, violent, and devious to boot.

The popularity of the idea of a patriarchal takeover of matriarchal societies in the Bronze Age and the notion of Minoan Crete as a last bastion of female power also influenced many other works beside historical novels. A visual example appears in *The Dinner Party* (1974–9) by the renowned American artist Judy Chicago,[55] which has been dubbed 'the most famous feminist artwork of all time'.[56] Chicago's artwork consists of a table in the shape of an open triangle, with 39 place settings. Each celebrates a mythical or historical woman, and one is devoted to the 'snake goddess' from Knossos. As explained in the accompanying 'Heritage Panels', Chicago explicitly refers to the patriarchal takeover in the section next to the image of the famous Knossian figurine brandishing snakes.[57]

---

[54] A slightly earlier novel that presents Minoan Crete as ripped apart by religious/political factions at the time of the Thera eruption and divided into similar lines is Moyra Caldecott's *The Lily and the Bull* (1979), which is suffused by New Age spiritualism and, unlike most novels about the decline of Minoan Crete, does not involve Mycenaean misdeeds in the Cretan misfortunes and focuses on the site of Malia instead of Knossos (Momigliano, 2020: 204–5).

[55] www.brooklynmuseum.org/exhibitions/dinner_party/

[56] https://news.artnet.com/exhibitions/the-brooklyn-museum-judy-chicago-dinner-party-1131506

[57] See www.brooklynmuseum.org/eascfa/dinner_party/place_settings/snake_goddess and www.brooklynmuseum.org/eascfa/dinner_party/heritage_panels/

Mycenaeans as patriarchal oppressors also appear in the influential socio-logical-historical essay and international bestseller *The Chalice and The Blade: Our History, Our Future* (1987) by Riane Eisler and in the amusing detective novel *The Players come Again* (1990) by Amanda Cross (nom de plume of Carolyne Heilbrun, a feminist professor of English at Columbia University).

The Chalice and The Blade offers a multi-disciplinary discussion of the evolution from peaceful to violent societies from prehistory to the present, in which Minoan Crete features as an example of a 'gylany', a term coined by Eisler in this book to indicate a type of society in which gender relations are not hierarchical but understood in terms of partnership. Minoan Crete is portrayed as a last bastion of this kind of society until conquered by Mycenaean patriarchal warlords (Eisler, 1987: 108–9).

In *The Players Come Again*, English professor and amateur detective Kate Fansler discovers family secrets while researching the biography of Gabrielle Foxx, the obscure wife of the famous writer Emmanuel Foxx, who is rumoured to have penned her husband's *Ariadne*, a masterpiece of modernist literature published in the early 1920s. Fansler does not find evidence that confirms this rumour, but she discovers, instead, a manuscript by Gabrielle, which is a 'a kind of counter novel to Emmanuel Foxx's *Ariadne*' and 'attempts to subvert, hell, to show up Emmanuel Foxx's masterpiece, to say nothing of bringing into question the whole masculine bias of high modernism' (Cross, 1990: 208 and 215). Fansler notes that while Emmanuel Foxx's plot 'depended on but neither admitted nor expounded its Greek original, Gabrielle's began with the exact prehistoric moment at which the Greek myth began' (Cross, 1990: 203). Besides, Fansler admires the way in which Gabrielle interweaves the results of archaeological discoveries in her narrative and 'must have read every morsel by Evans about his discoveries of the ancient Cretan civilization', unlike, one suspects, her husband (Cross, 1990: 202). Yet, there is little doubt that, despite mentioning Evans many times, this novel owes more to feminist literature than anything penned by the English archaeologist, since we learn that Gabrielle's Crete was a pacifist paradise, ruled by a queen, where gender equality reigned supreme – something that does not quite match Evans' priest-kings, their military conquests and (at times) oppressive thalassocracy (see e.g. Evans, 1921: 1–2). Instead, it recalls Eisler's gylany and Gimbutas' Kurgan hypothesis: 'Crete was a civilization that feared the violence and brutality of foreign men. Crete was a matriarchy, in the sense that the priests and the queen were women; but its men flourished as well: they were neither slaves nor concubines nor housekeepers' (Cross, 1990: 202). By contrast, 'Greek

men were violent: rapists, triumphant over women and weaker men when-
ever possible … Theseus might kill her [Ariadne's] whole family, seize
her double axe, and murder everyone along with the Minotaur' (Cross,
1990: 202).

Similar influences also appear in an intriguing Aegeomanic cultural practice of this period, namely Carol P. Christ's Goddess pilgrimage tours on
Crete, which were still going strong as late as 2022, despite Christ's passing
away in 2021. In her autobiographical essays, *Odyssey with the Goddess*
(1995) and *A Serpentine Path: Mysteries of the Goddess* (2016), Christ
described the path that led her to the creation of these pilgrimages and how
these transformed her life, while the tours website explains that the partici-
pants are offered lectures on Crete and the Goddess, visit museums and
archaeological sites, take part in sacred rituals inspired by Minoan Crete,
and are expected to 'learn about a Society of Peace where Goddess was
revered as the Source of Life, women were honored, people lived in harmony
with nature, and there was no war'.[58]

6.4 Cycladic Haute Couture and Aegeomania

Besides the enduring fascination provided by the perceived opposition
between Minoans and Mycenaeans, the spectacular archaeological discoveries at Akrotiri on Santorini/Thera have continued to stimulate recurring
bouts of Aegeomania. The role of the eruption of the Santorini volcano in
the decline and fall of the Minoans has fascinated scholars and laypersons
alike since the Greek archaeologist Spyridon Marinatos (1939) published
an article in which he suggested that the glory that was Crete was extin-
guished by this geological event (and the accompanying tsunamis and
ashfall). Although Marinatos' excavations on Thera in the late 1960s–
early 1970s (as well as excavations on Crete and other Aegean regions)
did not provide evidence for a sudden, catastrophic demise of Minoan
culture contemporary with the eruption, his astonishing finds, the frescoes
in particular, captured many people's imagination. For example, the
art historian and conservation-restoration theorist Cesare Brandi (cf.
Section 5.2), writing in the mid 1970s, commented very appreciatively on
the Akrotiri frescoes, which he considered much superior to those from
Knossos (Brandi, 2006 [1954]: 177–91, originally published in the daily
newspaper *Corriere della Sera* in 1975). But perhaps one of the best
illustrations of this appreciation of the Cycladic frescoes are some of the
luminous and ethereal garments in the spring–summer collection created by

---

[58] www.goddessariadne.org.

PATRIMOINE CHLOÉ 1084 (FACE) 1994 PE KARL LAGERFELD

Figure 23 Dress inspired by the Thera frescoes created by Karl Lagerfeld for the Chloé spring–summer 1994 collection (photo courtesy of Chloé; © Chloé. Exclusive property of Chloé SAS – **Reproduction prohibited**). See also video at https://www.youtube.com/watch?v=O3YIZ2PAt6I especially from 14' 40" onwards.

Karl Lagerfeld for the French fashion house Chloé in 1994 (Figures 23–24; for other examples see Boucher & Krapf, 2014: 198–9, catalogue nos. 320–2). Not only do these garments use motifs from the Akrotiri frescoes,

Figure 24 Sketch of dress illustrated in Figure 23 (photo courtesy of Chloé;
© Chloé. Exclusive property of Chloé SAS – **Reproduction prohibited**).

but they were presented at the collection's premier against a background
that imitated the cracked surface of the white- plastered walls from
Akrotiri, upon which the frescoes were painted.[59]

---

[59] See video at www.youtube.com/watch?v=O3YIZ2PAt6I especially from 14' 40'' onwards.

7 Aegeomania in the Early 21st Century

7.1 Enduring Fascinations: from Greek Mythology vs. Aegean Bronze Age Realities to Catastrophes and Uses of Linear B

The first quarter of the 21st century has seen a notable surge in Aegeomania cases, partly thanks to the growth of the internet and world wide web. Yet, despite the considerable innovations created by new media and new social contexts, some Aegeomanic trends attested in the 20th century have also continued into the first decades of the new century and new millennium.

Enduring trends include the use of Aegean Bronze Age material culture to give historical and local colour to modern retellings of famous Greek myths. Examples of this are Peter Huby's *Pasiphae* (2000) and Jennifer Saint's *Ariadne* (2021), two novels that make some references to Minoan material culture and the Thera eruption (albeit rather sparse). Interesting allusions to Aegean Bronze Age elements, and an ironic nod to the old idea of a Mycenaean patriarchy overtaking a matriarchal Minoan stage, also appear in Margaret Atwood's *The Penelopiad* (2005), a modern retelling of the story of Odysseus' wife by the author of *The Handmaid's Tale*, which focuses on Penelope and the twelve maids hanged by Odysseus and Telemachus at the end of the Homeric *Odyssey*.

Beside the *Odyssey* and other ancient Greek texts, a 'crucial' source for Atwood was *The Greek Myths* by Robert Graves (1955) – an author whose Cretomania is well illustrated by his novel *Seven Days in New Crete* (1949). Regarding Aegean Bronze Age elements in *The Penelopiad*, Atwood mentions Minoan double axes (cf. second quote, below) and seems to describe a tourist's visit to an Aegean Bronze Age archaeological site (or museum?) and its souvenir shop, when her Penelope refers to:

> ... enormous palaces that have – strangely – no kings or queens in them. Endless processions of people in graceless clothing file through these palaces, staring at the gold cups and the silver bowls, which are not even used anymore. Then they go to a sort of market inside the palace and buy pictures of these things, or miniature versions of them that are not real silver and gold. This is why I say *trash*. (Atwood, 2018 [2005]: 26).

Regarding the old theme of matriarchy vs patriarchy (as well as more allusions to Minoan material culture), Atwood's Penelope refers, for example, to Odysseus' 'newfangled idea that the wife should go to the husband's family rather than the other way around' (Atwood, 2018 [2005]: 37), while the twelve maids, in a chapter titled 'An anthropology lecture', reflect on the significance of their number and suggest that:

... our rape and subsequent hanging represent the overthrow of a matrilineal moon-cult by an incoming group of usurping patriarchal father-god worshipping barbarians. The chief of them, notably Odysseus, would then claim kingship by marrying the High Priestess of our cult, namely Penelope ... we deny that this theory is merely unfounded feminist claptrap ... Surely those axes, so significantly not used as weapons in the ensuing slaughter ... must have been the double-bladed ritual labrys axes associated with the Great Mother cult among the Minoans, the axes used to lop off the head of the Year King at the end of his term ... Point being that you don't have to get too worked up about us, dear educated minds. You do not have to think of us as real girls, real flesh and blood, real pain, real injustice. That might be too upsetting. Just discard the sordid part. Consider us pure symbol. (Atwood, 2018[2005]: 165–8).

Allusions to Aegean Bronze Age elements and questioning of later Greek myths also appear in the visual and performing arts. Examples are Roussetos Panagiotakis' almost Daliesque painting *Minotaur* (2014), which suggests that ancient Greek myths are stitched over and obscure an older Minoan reality (Figure 25) (personal communication); the 2011 production of Mozart's opera *Idomeneo* by Opera San Jose;[60] and Harrison Birtwistle's 2008 opera *Minotaur*, with libretto by David Harsent. The latter opera focuses on the inner world of

Figure 25 Roussetos Panagiotakis, *Minotaur* (2014) (photo courtesy of the artist).

---

[60] For images see www.shomler.com/osj/idomeneo/

Figure 26 Screenshot from a DVD of Birtwistle's 2008 opera *Minotaur*, published by Opus Arte (Catalogue no. OA 1000D; photo: Bill Cooper), showing the 'Snake Priestess' in the centre, between Ariadne and a priest.

the Minotaur himself (arguably the real hero in this retelling of the Greek myth), who is trapped in his narrow labyrinthine world and ultimately exploited for their own selfish goals by Theseus and Ariadne (who, like her stepbrother, feels imprisoned, and wishes to escape from Crete). This opera alludes to the Minoan past and material culture through its use of a gigantic 'Snake Priestess' modelled on the famous 'snake goddess' figurines from Knossos (Figure 26), whose part is sung by a countertenor. When I interviewed Birtwistle in 2015 and asked him about his use of this Minoan image, its imposing size, and the casting of a countertenor, he commented that he was guided, above all, by his desire to

Figure 27 Barbie dolls dressed like the famous 'Snake Goddess' figurines
found by Evans at Knossos in 1903 (photo courtesy of Maria Teresa Satta,
creator of these Barbie doll costumes).

create a wondrous theatrical effect (Momigliano, 2020: 235–6). But our conversation also revealed that Birtwistle perceived the Knossian 'snake goddess'
figurines as unrealistic exaggerations of the female body, with preposterously
long legs and enhanced breast, like a Barbie doll, and so he matched the
perceived exaggerated femaleness with the use of a countertenor, because he
considered this type of voice as more womanly than a woman's.

In this context, I should like to mention Maria Teresa Satta's use of Barbie dolls
for modelling her recreations of ancient female garments, many of which are
inspired by the material culture of the Aegean Bronze Age, from the Knossian
'snake goddess' figurines to the frescoes from Akrotiri (Figure 27).[61] Besides,
Barbie dolls have been used in connection with the Aegean Bronze Age in rather
more startling ways (Figures 28 and 29). All this and Birtwistle's perception of
the Knossian 'snake goddess' figurines should remind one of female sexual
objectification and the construction of female bodies; and should also prompt
us to ask questions about the creators and the users/viewers of this ancient and

---

[61] See also www.pinterest.com/pin/138696863517958636/; https://pin.it/4q1aOnG

Figure 28 Screenshot of 'snake goddess' figurine sold on Etsy by Sarah Franz-Wichlacz, owner of 'Witchcrafting' (see www.etsy.com/uk/listing/293403363/digital-download-minoan-snake-goddess)

Figure 29 'Ancient Minoan Culture illustrated with Barbies': screenshot from the website weird universe blog, August 2012: www.weirduniverse.net/blog/comments/ancient_minoan_culture_illustrated_with_barbies/

modern imagery as well as whether notions of male/female gaze might be usefully employed to explore Aegean Bronze Age iconography.

Beside the intersections between the material culture of the Aegean Bronze Age and later Greek mythology, another trend that continues into the 21st century is a fascination and creative engagement with the Aegean Bronze Age scripts.[62] Apart from the allusions to Linear A, Linear B, and the Phaistos disk in the latest Indiana Jones film (*Indiana Jones and the Dial of Destiny*, 2023),[63] an excellent example of this is the work of Greek artist Nikos Samartzidis, who employs Linear B in a variety of media, reminding his viewers of the 'Skripturale Malerei' of earlier generations, but with a contemporary twist. Samartzidis renders ancient and modern Greek lyrics (from Homer to Odysseus Elytis and Greek singer-songwriter Dionysis Savvopoulos) into Linear B and then onto paintings, clay tablets, and other media. He has also used lyrics by the musician and Nobel-laureate Bob Dylan rendered in Linear B, as illustrated in Figure 30.[64] As shown in the next Section (7.2) on Aegeomania and modern catastrophes, the disappearance and rediscovery of Linear B also plays a part in Sally Rooney's novel *Beautiful World, Where Are You* (2021).

The few examples mentioned above will suffice to illustrate that, even if some Aegeomanic trends and practices have a very long history, every new generation establishes new dialogues with the inhabitants of the Bronze Age Aegean and their material culture. These dialogues are often prompted and informed by the latest discoveries and theories in various disciplines, but above all by the preoccupations and desires of different individuals and groups: to paraphrase Joseph de Maistre (1853: 264) and Jacquetta Hawkes (1967: 174), one could argue that 'Every Age has the Aegean Bronze Age it deserves and desires'. In the 21st century, this adaptability of the Aegean Bronze Age as a mirror for the concerns of individuals and groups is also shown by some new developments. One that seems to me characteristic of our times is the use of Aegean Bronze Age archaeology (especially the Bronze Age eruption of

---

[62] Alongside the work of Samartzidis, discussed below, I would also like to mention the memorial project titled 'Linear B' and devoted to the Greek artist Nikos Alexiou, which was curated by Christina Mitrentse and Jonas Ranson in 2011 at the Stephen Lawrence Gallery in London (see: https://alexioulinearb.wordpress.com/).

[63] https://diggingupthepast.substack.com/p/indiana-jones-and-the-dial-of-destiny

[64] See also https://sites.utexas.edu/scripts/2018/02/28/paintings-and-poetry-in-linear-b-the-nikos-samartzidis-collection/; https://sites.utexas.edu/scripts/2022/03/11/dylanology-i-ii-iii/ and the artist's website www.nikosam-art.de/.

Figure 30 Nikos Samartzidis, *Dilanology II* (2017), which is inspired by Linear B and Bob Dylan's song 'Blowin' in the wind'. It is part of a triptych that uses lyrics from Dylan's songs translated into modern Greek and then written in Linear B (photo courtesy of the artist).

Santorini) to reflect upon contemporary cataclysms and catastrophes – from climate change and related environmental disasters to various financial crises and the recent Covid 19 pandemic – and their effects on societies and individuals. All these calamities seem to have turned the attention of some artists and writers to the Aegean Bronze Age past as a catalyst for reflection on these topical issues, as illustrated below.

7.2 Aegeomanic Catastrophes – From Global to Personal Disasters

In 2014, Giant Squid, a post-metal progressive rock band from California formed in the early 2000s, but inactive since 2015, produced what may be its swan song, the album *Minoans*.[65] This, in the words of Aaron John Gregory, one of the band's founders, was a 'love letter to the Mediterranean and specifically Bronze-age Greece . . . which I feel mirrors these heartbreakingly brutal, turbulent times we live in today'.[66] As the album lyrics and interviews released by Gregory illustrate, the turbulences that he had in mind were the eruption of Santorini and the Mycenaean conquest of Minoan Crete in ancient times, and nuclear disasters and global warming in modern times.

The Minoans are presented by Gregory as a people suspended between East and West, who live in harmony with nature, especially with the sea; they are a naval power, but they are not warlike; although now largely forgotten, they are the origins of European civilization because of the legacy they passed on to the Mycenaeans and, through the Mycenaeans, to the Greeks; they practiced cannibalism (an allusion to the children's bones with butchery marks found at Knossos in 1979: cf. Section 6.1), but only in exceptional circumstances. As hinted at in the song 'Mycenaeans', cannibalism was the result of the penury and devastations caused by the Thera eruption and its aftermath, which eventually led to the Mycenaean conquest of Crete: 'What will the Greeks think when they see what we've become? / Delusion, chaos, and cannibalism'. The song 'Phaistos Disk' also alludes to Minoan cannibalism and presents the disk as the record of a great catastrophe caused by the sea and an admonition to future generations: 'Let the disc illustrate, / why our children's bones are flayed . . . Let the disc serve as warning / Never unearth these graves'. The song 'Palace of Knossos' evokes the feeling of obliteration, fragility, and impermanence experienced by its inhabitants after the catastrophe: 'We will be forgotten, we will be lost / A sunken island, legend to none'. The effects of the tsunamis connected with the Thera eruption are also evoked in 'Sixty Foot Waves', which, according to Gregory, besides its historical reference, can also be interpreted metaphorically as a prophecy of what might happen to our contemporary coastal towns if hit by tsunamis, especially in the light of rising ocean levels and the Fukushima Daiichi nuclear disaster of March 2011.[67] In fact, the whole album can be understood literally and metaphorically as an elegy for the downfall of the Minoans but also for the timeless

---

[65] https://giantsquid.bandcamp.com/album/minoans

[66] Interview with Gregory in *Burning Ambulance* available at https://burningambulance.com/2014/10/21/premiere-giant-squid/.

[67] Interview with Gregory (see note 66).

feelings of impermanence and loss that can be experienced at any time, when humanity confronts natural and man-made disasters.

Another Aegeomanic work that focuses on the Bronze Age eruption of Santorini and the intersections between natural/man-made cataclysms, Mediterranean societies and their history, as well as individual lives is Zeruya Shalev's *Thera*, first published in Hebrew in 2005 and translated into English in 2010. In this novel, the Thera eruption is linked to disasters described in the Old Testament, namely to the theory that it triggered the plagues of Egypt and the subsequent Jewish exodus – a theory that, for various reasons, has exercised cranks and serious scholars alike for decades (see e.g. Geraty, 2015 and Harris, 2015, with further references).[68]

Most importantly, in the context of the novel, the Thera eruption and its aftermath are linked, metaphorically, to a personal disaster in the lives of the main characters: the divorce between the protagonist and narrator, Ella, and her husband Amnon, with all the effects that this has on their lives and on that of their only child, Gili.

Ella and Amnon are Israeli archaeologists who live in Jerusalem. Ella looks like the famous Minoan fresco known as 'La Parisienne',[69] which, with poetic licence, is described in the novel as a find from the site of Akrotiri on Thera, rather than Knossos. Amnon, on first meeting Ella, remarks: ' ... I've seen you before, you've been painted on the wall in Thera, in the Minoan site, they call you the Parisian ... you've existed for four thousand years' (Shalev, 2010: 71).

While her marriage flounders, Ella conducts research on the links between Thera and Jewish history, even though her father had warned her that 'the correlation between Thera and the exodus from Egypt is currently considered to be wholly unscientific' (Shalev, 2010: 141). Nevertheless, Ella continues to be fascinated by this event and by the effects of major cataclysms on individual people, who are traumatized, displaced, and whose familiar worlds and old certainties collapse. Throughout the novel, various archaeological images and

---

[68] An earlier Israeli novel that intersects the Aegean Bronze Age with Jewish history is A. B. Yehoshua *Mr Mani* (first published in Hebrew in 1989; Yehoshua, 1992). In this remarkable work, Yehoshua refers to Minoan Crete in a chapter that discusses an important crossroad in Jewish history, the Shoah during World War II, which is represented by the battle of Crete and its aftermath. Yehoshua uses Minoan Crete, ironically, as the origins of Europe but also as the opposite of the present: he suggests that Hitler sent his best troops to bleed to death on Crete simply to let Europe know that his long arm could reach the roots it grew from. He also presents Minoan Crete as an ancient blissful civilization, not only because of its apparent peacefulness, but also because Jewishness had not yet been invented. In a sense, for Yehoshua Minoan Crete and its alleged pacifism are a cue to reflect upon the complexity of various identities –Jewish, German, Arab, Mediterranean, and European.

[69] See www.heraklionmuseum.gr/en/exhibit/la-parisienne-fresco/

especially the Thera eruption become metaphors to describe Ella's divorce and its effects. Thus, for example, her decision to divorce is compared to a 'catastrophe' (Shalev, 2010: 19), of which the 'consequences will reverberate ... like that volcanic eruption' (Shalev, 2010: 122). Furthermore, the divorce itself is described as 'an explosion whose ashes would cover the sun for months on end' (Shalev, 2010: 124), while some months after her separation and divorce, Ella reflects that she is trying to reconstruct 'the story of Thera as if it were a painful childhood memory', as if it belonged to her 'former life' (Shalev, 2010: 314).

Aegean Bronze Age disasters, their effects on individuals, and their topicality in an uncertain world also appear in *Beautiful World, Where Are You* (2021), by the Irish author Sally Rooney. The novel is set in present times (c. 2019–20) and is mostly about love among people aged in their late twenties–early thirties, living in Ireland, and feeling that the world is experiencing a major crisis, or is even 'on the cusp of extinction' (Rooney, 2021: 138). Among the symptoms of this crisis are the upsurge of right-wing politicians and their inept policies towards the environmental crisis, climate change, pollution, world poverty, and mass drowning of refugees, among other things. Little do the characters in the novel know, for most of the story, that their world is on the brink of the Covid 19 pandemic, but the final two chapters are, in fact, set in the middle of the first lockdown of 2020.

This feeling of living in a period of unprecedented crisis (even before the Covid 19 pandemic) leads the two main female characters – Alice and Eileen – to delve into the Late Bronze Age 'collapse of civilization'. Thus, in an email to Alice, Eileen writes:

> Apparently in the Late Bronze Age, starting about 1,500 years before the Christian era, the Eastern Mediterranean region was characterised by a system of centralised palace governments ... Then, during a seventy-five-year period from about 1225 to 1150 BC, civilisation collapsed. ... Literacy all but died out, and entire writing systems were lost. No one is sure why any of this happened ... Wikipedia suggests a theory called 'general system collapse' ... Another of the theories is headlined simply: 'Climate change'. I think this puts our present civilisation in a kind of ominous light, don't you? ... Considering the approaching civilisation collapse maybe you think children are out of the question anyway. (Rooney, 2021: 40–1).

On reading this email, Alice, who is a successful novelist, becomes particularly intrigued by one aspect of this collapse, namely the complete loss of writing systems. This prompts her to learn more about Linear B, and in her response to Eileen she expatiates on the discovery of Linear B tablets at Knossos and Pylos, mentions Arthur Evans, Michael Ventris, John Chadwick, and Alice Kober

(Rooney, 2021: 56–8), and offers some reflections on the relationship between past and present:

> I have been thinking lately about the ancient world coming back to us, emerging through strange ruptures in time, through the colossal speed and waste and godlessness of the twentieth century, through the hands and eyes of Alice Kober, a chain-smoker dead at forty-three, and Michael Ventris, dead in a car crash at the age of thirty-four . . . during the Bronze Age, a sophisticated syllabic script was developed to represent the Greek language in writing, and then during the collapse you told me about, all that knowledge was completely destroyed. Later writing systems devised to represent Greek bear no relation to Linear B. The people who developed and used them had no idea that Linear B had ever even existed. The unbearable thing is that when first inscribed, those markings meant something to the people who wrote and read them, and then for thousands of years they meant nothing, nothing, nothing – because the link was broken, history had stopped. And then the twentieth century shook the watch and made history happen again. But can't we do that too, in another way? (Rooney, 2021: 58).

Eileen adds to these reflections by commenting on the effects of collapse of 'civilisation' on poor people, which she thinks were not as dramatic as often portrayed:

> But how many people, how many inhabitants of this 'civilisation' actually lived in palaces? How many wore the jewellery, drank from the bronze cups, ate the pomegranates? For every one member of the elite, thousands more were illiterate and impoverished subsistence farmers. After the 'collapse of civilisation', many of them moved elsewhere, and some may have died, but for the most part their lives probably did not change much. They went on growing crops. Sometimes the harvest was good and sometimes it wasn't. And in another corner of the continent, those people were your ancestors and mine – not the palace-dwellers. (Rooney, 2021: 160).

These ideas chime with existing Marxist or quasi-Marxist interpretations of the fall of the Aegean palaces, which suggest that this represented an improvement for most of the population as it was a liberation from despotic rulers (cf. 1 Introduction). But the collapse of 'civilisation' also prompts Eileen to ask: 'What if the meaning of life on earth is not eternal progress towards some unspecified goal – the engineering and production of more and more powerful technologies, the development of more abstruse and complex cultural forms? What if these things just rise and recede naturally, like tides, while the meaning of life remains the same always – just to live and be with other people?' (Rooney, 2021: 161).

As Rooney's book was published in 2021, the ideas that poor, subsistence farmers survive catastrophes and especially that the meaning of life is 'to live and be with other people' strongly resonated with the feelings of many individuals who had just experienced the lockdowns of the Covid 19 pandemic and the death of loved ones. It also seems to be part of Rooney's strategy to end the book on a positive note, with a celebration of life and friendship. While sympathizing with Rooney's focus on the Aegean Bronze Age lower classes and her desire to offer an uplifting end to her novel, one may perhaps reflect more critically on the unchanging life of peasants and lower classes generally (even in the Aegean Bronze Age), since one of the many things that the Covid 19 pandemic has brought to the fore is how some catastrophes and collapses can have more devastating effects on poor people and poor countries, whereas some rich individuals and corporate groups only seem to increase their profits.

7.3 Conclusions

The phenomenon of Aegeomania – defined as the use of Aegean Bronze Age material culture in various cultural practices, from literature to the performing arts, to create something new – can be traced back to the last quarter of the 19th century and was sparked by Schliemann's archaeological discoveries at Troy, Mycenae, and other Aegean sites. It is, however, the rediscovery of Minoan Crete in the early 20th century, with the emergence of the highly virulent Cretomania variant, which created the first serious outbreak of Aegeomania, and was largely facilitated by the perceived affinities between Minoan and early modernist art. Since then, Aegeomania has persisted to the present day through its different variants, including the Cycladic strain that grew in the interwar period.

Aegeomania and its variants have developed and mutated over the last century and a half, reaching an ever-wider variety of people, cultural practices, and genres. In the beginning, during the late Belle Époque, this phenomenon seems to have been largely circumscribed to avant-garde writers and artists, especially those linked to Paris, the cultural capital of the world at that time, such as those gravitating in the orbit of the revolutionary Ballets Russes. By the interwar period, however, Aegeomania had spread even to Mills & Boon romances and the furnishings created by Swedish and French interior design companies.

Many new cultural practices affected by Aegeomania have developed since World War II and future generations will undoubtedly create new ones. If the Aegean Bronze Age mattered to non-specialists in the Belle Époque, and has continued to matter to the present day, it is because the archaeological discoveries and their interpretations have been incorporated into contemporary debates ranging from the development of social organizations and gender relations (matriarchy, patriarchy, gylany) to the construction of modern identities at local (e.g. Cretan), regional (e.g. Hellenic), and transnational (e.g. European) level, since Minoans and Mycenaeans have often been invoked in narratives of European origins (e.g. Davies, 1996: 81, ' ..it is now generally accepted that Minoan culture on Crete, and Mycenaean culture on mainland Greece, formed the twin peaks of "Europe's first civilization"').

Many examples of Aegeomanic practices have been discussed in previous publications (e.g. Farnoux, 1993, 1996a, 1996b; Cadogan, 2004; Hamilakis & Momigliano, 2006; Momigliano & Farnoux, 2017; Momigliano, 2020) and in this essay. Nevertheless, I am only too conscious that, in this essay, my focus is largely Eurocentric, that I have barely touched upon some genres, and that I have effectively ignored others, such as comics, of which Eric Shanower 'Age of Bronze Aeries' is a shining example.[70] This is not because I consider these insignificant, but for mere lack of time and space. One intriguing genre that seems to me to have been overlooked so far, but I suspect could repay systematic research, is that of video games. These have recently become the focus of scholarly attention, because of their increasing importance in everyday life, as illustrated, for example, by the publication of a 'Video Games Research Framework' issued by the UK government on 30 May 2023,[71] by recent scholarly volumes on videogames and Classical antiquity (e.g. Rollinger, 2020; Clare, 2021), and by their inclusion in museum exhibitions (e.g. *Assassin's Creed Odyssey-Knossos Palace* in the 2023 Ashmolean Museum exhibition 'Labyrinth: Knossos, myth and reality': see Shapland, 2023).

Despite its omissions, I hope that this essay will be a useful primer for Aegeomania – a phenomenon that scholars and students alike should not dismiss as irrelevant to the study of the Aegean Bronze Age, for a variety of reasons, such as those mentioned in the Introduction. Although visiting Aegean sites and museums as well as reading traditional archaeological books are the fundamental activities for gaining familiarity with the Aegean Bronze Age, understanding the connection between Aegeomania and the devastation of archaeological sites as well as some appreciation of works such as D'Annunzio's *La Città Morta* or Renault's *The King Must Die* can also offer useful insights into the history of this discipline. Aegeomania can help us to reflect upon different approaches and biases in the studies of the Aegean

---

[70] http://age-of-bronze.com/ and www.ericshanower.com/. On comics that refer to the Aegean Bronze Age, especially Minoan Crete, see also e.g. Driessen (2017); Momigliano (2020: 183, 221–2, 233). Boucher & Krapf (2014) also refer to Japanese manga.

[71] www.gov.uk/government/publications/video-games-research-framework/video-games-research-framework

Bronze Age, including our own, because (paraphrasing an Egyptologist's words) there is no definitive Aegean Bronze Age: 'the material remains of the past are always interpreted through the concerns of the present and filtered through layers of cultural memory'; when we search for the Aegean Bronze Age 'we cannot help but find ourselves' (Riggs, 2017: 189).

References

Ackroyd, P. (2006). *The Fall of Troy: A Novel*. London: Chatto & Windus.

Anderson, P. (1971). *The Dancer from Atlantis*. New York: Doubleday.

Andronikos, M. (1954). Η "Δωρική Εισβολή" και τα αρχαιολογικά ευρήματα. *Hellenika* 13, 221–40.

Armstrong, R. H. (2005). *A Compulsion for Antiquity: Freud and the Ancient World*. Ithaca, NY: Cornell University Press.

Atwood, M. (2018 [2005]). *The Penelopiad*. Edinburgh: Canongate.

Ayrton, M. (2015 [1967]). *The Maze Maker*. Chicago: University of Chicago Press.

Bach, F. T. (2006). *Shaping the Beginning. Modern Artists and the Ancient Eastern Mediterranean*. Athens: N. P. Goulandris Foundation–Museum of Cycladic Art.

Bailey, D. (2015). Art//Archaeology//Art: Letting-Go Beyond. In I. Russell and A. Cochrane, eds., *Art and Archaeology: Collaborations, Conversations, Criticisms*. New York: Springer, pp. 231–50.

Bailey, D. (2017). Art/Archaeology: What Value Artistic-Archaeological Collaborations? *Journal of Contemporary Archaeology*, 4(2), 246–56.

Bann, S. (1967). *Concrete Poetry: An International Anthology*. London: London Magazine Editions.

Bayen, B. (1982). *Schliemann, Épisodes Ignorés*. Paris: Gallimard.

Beaton, R. (1995). *Ariadne's Children*. London: Weidenfeld and Nicolson.

Beaton, R. (2006). Minoans in Modern Greek Literature. In Y. Hamilakis and N. Momigliano, eds., *Archaeology and European Modernity: Producing and Consuming the 'Minoans'*. Padova: Bottega d'Erasmo (Ausilio), pp. 183–95.

Beaton, R. (2008). Kazantzakis the Cretan: Versions of the Minoan Past from the Author of *Zorba the Greek*. *Kampos: Cambridge Studies in Modern Greek*, 16, 1–23.

Bennett, T. and Joyce, P. (2010). *Material Powers: Cultural Studies, History and the Material Turn*. London: Routledge.

Berry, E. (1933). *The Winged Girl of Knossos*. New York: D. Appelton.

Bintliff, J. (1984). Structuralism and Myth in Minoan Studies. *Antiquity*, 58(222), 33–8.

Birtacha, K. (2016). Examining the Paint on Cycladic Figurines. In M. Marthari, C. Renfrew, and M. J. Boyd, eds., *Early Cycladic Sculpture in Context*. Oxford: Oxbow Books, pp. 491–502.

Blakolmer, F. (2006). The Arts of Bronze Age Crete and the European Modern Style: Reflecting and Shaping Different Identities. In Y. Hamilakis and N. Momigliano, eds., *Archaeology and European Modernity: Producing and Consuming the 'Minoans'*. Padova: Bottega d'Erasmo (Ausilio), pp. 219–40.

Blakolmer, F. (2010). Images and Perceptions of the Lion Gate Relief at Mycenae During the 19th Century. In F. Buscemi, ed., *Cogitata tradere posteris. The Representation of Ancient Architecture in the XIXth Century*. Rome: Bonanno, pp. 49–66.

Blegen, C. W, Caskey, J. L., Rawson, M. and Sperling, J. (1950). *Troy. General Introduction. The First and Second Settlements*. Princeton, NJ: University Press for University of Cincinnati.

Blegen, C. W., Boulter, C. G., Caskey, J. L. and Rawson, M. (1958). *Troy: Settlements VIIa, VIIb and VIII*. Princeton, NJ: Princeton University Press for the University of Cincinnati.

Bossert, H. T. (1921). *Alt Kreta. Kunst und Kunstgewerbe im Ägäischen Kulturkreise*. Berlin: Ernst Wasmuth.

Boucher, A. (2017). The Ocean-liner Aramis: A Voyage to the Land of Minos and Art Deco. In N. Momigliano and A. Farnoux, eds., *Cretomania: Modern Desires for the Minoan Past*. London: Routledge, pp. 124–56.

Boucher, A. and Krapf, T. (2014). Des Jeux Olympiques aux Mangas Japonais: l'Art Égéenne est Partout. In A. Boucher, ed., *La Grèce des origines: entre rêve et archéologie*. Paris: Réunion des Musées Nationaux – Grand Palais, pp. 195–99.

Bourke, L. (2014). The Image of the Minoan in Science Fiction. *Foundation: The International Review of Science Fiction*, 43(118), 9–18.

Brandi, C. (2006 [1954]). *Viaggio nella Grecia Antica*, 3rd edition, with preface by E. Siciliano. Roma: Editori Riuniti.

Brindel, J. R. (1980). *Ariadne*. New York: St Martin's Press.

Brindel, J. R. (1985). *Phaedra*. New York: St Martin's Press.

Brinkmann, V. (2017). *Gods in Color. Polychromy in the Ancient World*. Munich: Fine Arts Museums of San Francisco and DelMonico Books.

Brown, D. (2003). *The Da Vinci Code*. New York: Doubleday.

Burke, J. (2006a). *The Gods of Freud: Sigmund Freud's Art Collection*. New York: Knopf.

Burke, J. (2006b). *The Sphinx on the Table: Sigmund Freud's Art Collection and the Development of Psychoanalysis*. New York: Walker and Company.

Burns, B. E. (2010). *Mycenaean Greece, Mycenaean Commerce, and The Formation of Identity*. Cambridge: Cambridge University Press.

Buscemi, F. (2010). Il cd. Tesoro di Atreo a Micene: prime indagini e restituzioni inedite. In F. Buscemi, ed., *Cogitata tradere posteris. The Representation of Ancient Architecture in the XIXth Century*. Rome: Bonanno, pp. 67–86.

Cadogan, G. (2004). 'The Minoan Distance': the Impact of Knossos Upon the Twentieth Century. In G. Cadogan, E. Hatzaki, and A. Vasilakis, eds., *Knossos: Palace, City, State. Proceedings of the Conference in Herakleion organised by the British School at Athens and the 23rd Ephoreia of Prehistoric and Classical Antiquities of Herakleion, in November 2000, for the Centenary of Sir Arthur Evans's Excavations at Knossos.* London: British School at Athens, pp. 537–45.

Caldecott, M. (1979). *The Lily and the Bull.* London: Rex Collings.

Caloi, I. (2011). *Modernità Minoica. L'arte Egea e l'Art Nouveau: il caso di Mariano Fortuny y Madrazo.* Florence: Florence University Press.

Caloi, I. (2017). The Minoan Woman as the Oriental Woman: Mariano Fortuny's Knossos Scarves and Ruth St. Denis. In N. Momigliano and A. Farnoux, eds., *Cretomania: Modern Desires for the Minoan Past.* London : Routledge, pp. 71–83.

Castleden, R. (1990). *Minoans: Life in Bronze Age Crete.* London: Routledge.

Chadwick, J. (1976). Who were the Dorians? *La parola del passato*, 31, 103–17.

Chryssovitsanou, V. (2004). Les figurines cycladiques: de la répulsion à la fascination. In S. Basch, ed., *La métamorphose des ruines: l'influence des découvertes archéologiques sur les arts et les lettres, 1870–1914.* Athens: École française d'Athènes, pp. 33–8.

Chryssovitsanou, V. (2006). Les statuettes cycladiques et l' art modern. In P. Darcque, M. Fotiadis, and O. Polychronopoulou, eds., *Mythos. La préhistoire Égeene du XIXe au XXIe siècle après J.-C. Table ronde internationale, 21–23 Novembre 2002.* Athens: École française d'Athènes, pp. 337–43.

Chryssovitsanou, V. (2013). Henry Moore et l'art cycladique. *Les nouvelles de l'archéologie*, 134, 5–11.

Clare, R. (2021). *Ancient Greece and Rome in Videogames. Representation, Play, Transmedia.* London: Bloomsbury.

Constantine, D. (1998). *The Pelt of Wasps.* Newcastle upon Tyne: Bloodaxe.

Crawford, S. (1983). Re-evaluating Material Culture: Crawling Towards a Reconstruction of Minoan Society. In O. Krzyszkowska and L. Nixon, eds., *Minoan Society: Proceedings of the Cambridge Colloquium, 1981.* Bristol: Bristol Classical Press, pp. 47–53.

Cross, A. (1990). *The Players Come Again.* New York: Random House.

Culler, J. (2013). Lévi-Strauss: Good to Think With. In R. Doran, ed., *Rethinking Claude Lévi-Strauss (1908–2009).* Yale French Studies 123. New Haven, CT: Yale University Press, pp. 6–13.

D'Agata, A. L. (1994). Sigmund Freud and Aegean Archaeology: Mycenaean and Cypriote Material from his Collection of Antiquities. *Studi Micenei ed Egeo-Anatolici*, 34, 7–41.

D'Annunzio, G. (1899). *La città morta*. Milan: Treves.

D'Annunzio, G. (1900). *Il Fuoco*. Milan: Treves.

Darling, J. K. (2004). *Architecture in Greece*. Westport, CT: Greenwood Press.

Davies, N. (1996). *Europe. A History*. Oxford: Oxford University Press.

DeLillo, D. (1982). *The Names*. New York: Alfred A. Knopf.

DeLillo, D. (2011 [1988]). The Ivory Acrobat. In Don DeLillo, *The Angel Esmeralda: Nine Stories*. London: Picador, pp. 55–72.

De Maistre, J. (1853). *Lettres et opuscules inédits du comte Joseph de Maistre, Tome 1 / précédés d'une notice biographique pars son fils le comte Rodolphe de Maistre*. Paris: Varon. (https://gallica.bnf.fr/ark:/12148/bpt6k246120/f3.item).

Driessen, J. (2017). In bulls doth the Earth-Shaker delight. In S. Jusseret and M. Sintubin, eds., *Minoan Earthquakes: Breaking the Myth through Interdisciplinarity*, Leuven: Leuven University Press, pp. 19–28.

Driessen, J. and Kalantzopoulou, T. (2024). *Taking Home Agamemnon: The Casts of the Lion Gate at Mycenae*, Louvain-la-Neuve: Presses universitaires de Louvain.

Durrell, L. (1947). *Cefalû. A Novel*. London: Editions Poetry.

Durrell, L. (1958). *The Dark Labyrinth: A Novel*. London: Faber.

Easton, D. F. (1998). Heinrich Schliemann: Hero or Fraud? *The Classical World*, 91(5), 335–43.

Eisler, R. T. (1987). *The Chalice and The Blade: Our History, Our Future*. San Francisco: Harper Collins.

Evans, A. J. (1901). The Palace of Knossos. Provisional Report of the Excavations for the Year 1901. *Annual of the British School at Athens*, 7, 1–120.

Evans, A. J. (1921). *The Palace of Minos: A Comparative Account of the Successive Stages of the Early Cretan Civilization as Illustrated by the Discoveries at Knossos, Vol. I*. London: Macmillan.

Evans, A. J. (1935). *The Palace of Minos: A Comparative Account of the Successive Stages of the Early Cretan Civilization as Illustrated by the Discoveries at Knossos, Vol. IV*. London: Macmillan.

Farnoux, A. (1993). *Cnossos: L'archéologie d'un rêve*. Paris: Gallimard.

Farnoux, A. (1996a). Art Minoenne et Art Nouveau. In P. Hoffmann and P. L. Rinui, eds., *Antiquités Imaginaires: La Référence Antique dans L'art Moderne, de la Renaissance à Nos Jours. Actes de la Table Ronde du 29 avril 1994*. Paris: École Normale Supérieure, pp. 109–26.

Farnoux, A. (1996b). *Knossos: Unearthing a Legend*. London: Thames and Hudson.

Farrer, K. (2004 [1954]). *The Cretan Counterfeit*. Boulder, CO: The Rue Morgue Press.

Finley, M. (1968). *Aspects of Antiquity*. London: Chatto & Windus.

Fitton, J. L. (1989). *Cycladic Art*. London: British Museum.

Fitton, J. L. (1995). *The Discovery of the Greek Bronze Age*. London: British Museum.

Florou, V. (2016). Anna Apostolaki: A Forgotten Pioneer of Women's Emancipation in Greece, *Archivist's Notebook*, 1 January 2016, https://natalia vogeikoff.com/2016/01/01/anna-apostolaki-a-forgotten-pioneer-of-womens-emancipation-in-greece.

Gell, W. (1810). *The Itinerary of Greece with a Commentary on Pausanias and Strabo and an Account of the Monuments of Antiquity at Present Existing in that Country*. London: T. Payne.

Geraty, L. T. (2015). Exodus Dates and Theories. In T. E. Levy, T. Schneider, and W. H. C. Propp, eds., *Israel's Exodus in Transdisciplinary Perspective: Text, Archaeology, Culture, and Geoscience*. Cham: Springer, pp. 55–64.

Gere, C. (2006). Cretan Psychoanalysis and Freudian Archaeology: H.D.'s Minoan Analysis with Freud in 1933. In Y. Hamilakis and N. Momigliano, eds., *Archaeology and European Modernity: Producing and Consuming the 'Minoans'*. Padova: Bottega d'Erasmo (Ausilio), pp. 211–18.

Gere, C. (2009). *Knossos and the Prophets of Modernism*. Chicago: The University of Chicago Press.

Getz-Preziosi, P. (1987). *Sculptors of the Cyclades. Individual and Tradition in the Third Millennium B.C.* Ann Arbor, MN: The University of Michigan Press.

Giannouli, A. (2012). D'une *Antigone* (1844) à l'autre (1893). In S. Humbert-Mougin and C. Lechevallier, eds., *Le théâtre antique entre France et Allemagne (XIXe-XXe siècles). De la traduction à la mise en scène*. Tours: Presses universitaires François-Rabelais (https://books.openedition.org/pufr/15575)

Gibbins, D. (2005). *Atlantis*. London: Headline.

Gibbins, D. (2010). *The Mask of Troy*. London: Headline.

Gill, D. W. J. and Chippindale, C. (1993). Material and Intellectual Consequences of Esteem for Cycladic Figures. *American Journal of Archaeology*, 97(4), 601–59.

Gimbutas, M. (1974). *The Gods and Goddesses of Old Europe, 7000 to 3500 BC: Myths, Legends and Cult Images*. London: Thames and Hudson.

Gimbutas, M. (1982). *The Goddesses and Gods of Old Europe, 6500–3500 BC: Myths and Cult Images*. London: Thames and Hudson.

Gimbutas, M. and M. R. Dexter (1999). *The Living Goddesses*. Berkeley, CA: University of California Press.

González-Vaquerizo, H. (2021). Kazantzakis's *Odyssey*: A (Post)modernist Sequel. *Journal of Modern Greek Studies*, 39(2), 349–77.

Graves, R. (1949). *Seven Days in New Crete*. London: Cassel and Co.

Graves, R. (1955). *The Greek Myths*. Harmondsworth: Penguin Books.

Green, R. L. (1957). *Mystery at Mycenae: An Adventure Story of Ancient Greece*. London: Bodley Head.

Green, R. L. (1961). *The Luck of Troy*. London: Bodley Head.

Greenberg, R. and Hamilakis, Y. (2022). *Archaeology, Nation, and Race: Confronting the Past, Decolonizing the Future in Greece and Israel*. Cambridge: Cambridge University Press.

Groenewegen-Frankfort, H. A. (1951). *Arrest and Movement: An Essay on Space and Time in the Representational Art of the Ancient Near East*. London: Faber & Faber.

Gudmundsson, K. (1937). *Gyðjan og uxinn: skáldsaga*. Reykjavík: Ólafur Erlingsson.

Gudmundsson, K. (1940). *Winged Citadel*, trans. by B. Mussey. New York: Henry Holt and Co.

Halstead, P. (1988). On redistribution and the Origin of Minoan–Mycenaean Palatial Economies. In E. B. French and K. A. Wardle, eds., *Problems in Greek Prehistory*. Bristol: Bristol Classical Press, pp. 519–30.

Hamilakis, Y. (2011). Indigenous Archaeologies in Ottoman Greece. In Z. Bahrani, Z. Çelik, and E. Eldem, eds., *Scramble for the Past: The Story of Archaeology in the Ottoman Empire 1733–1914*. Istanbul: Salt, pp. 49–69.

Hamilakis, Y. (2013). *Archaeology and the Senses: Human Experience, Memory, and Affect*. New York: Cambridge University Press.

Hamilakis, Y. and Momigliano, N. (2006). *Archaeology and European Modernity: Producing and Consuming the 'Minoans'*. Padova: Bottega d'Erasmo (Ausilio).

Hand, J. (2001 [1999]). *Voice of the Goddess*. Cardiff, CA: Pacific Rim Press.

Harloe, K. and Momigliano, N. (2018). Introduction. Hellenomania: Ancient and Modern Obsessions with the Greek Past. In K. Harloe, N. Momigliano, and A. Farnoux, eds., *Hellenomania*. London: Routledge, pp. 1–19.

Harris, M. (2015). The Thera Theories: Science and the Modern Reception History of the Exodus. In T. E. Levy, T. Schneider, and W. H. C. Propp, eds., *Israel's Exodus in Transdisciplinary Perspective: Text, Archaeology, Culture, and Geoscience*. Cham: Springer, pp. 91–9.

Hawkes, J. (1967). God in the Machine. *Antiquity*, 41, 174–80.

Hawkes, J. (1968). *Dawn of the Gods*. London: Chatto & Windus.

Hawkes, J. (1980). *Quest of Love*. London: Chatto & Windus.

Heidegger, M. (2005). *Sojourns. The Journey to Greece*, English trans. by J.P. Manoussakis. New York: State University of New York Press.

Hendrix, E. A. (2003). Painted Early Cycladic Figures: An Exploration of Context and Meaning. *Hesperia: The Journal of the American School of Classical Studies at Athens*, 72(4), 405–46.

Hicks, D. (2010). The Material-Cultural Turn: Event and Effect. In D. Hicks and M.C. Beaudry, eds., *The Oxford Handbook of Material Culture Studies*. Oxford: Oxford University Press, pp. 25–98.

Hobsbawm, E. (1994). *The Age of Extremes: The Short Twentieth Century, 1914–1991*. London: Michael Joseph.

Hodder, I. (2012). *Entangled: An Archaeology of the Relationships between Humans and Things*. Oxford: Wiley-Blackwell.

Hodne, L. (2022). The Primacy of Form Over Color: On the Discussion of Primary and Secondary Qualities in Herder's *Pygmalion*. *The Journal of Aesthetics and Art Criticism*, 80(3), 309–32.

Howes, D. (2006). *Empire of the Senses: The Sensual Culture Reader*. Oxford: Berg.

Howes, D. (2013). The Expanding Field of Sensory Studies, https://www.sensorystudies.org/sensorial-investigations/the-expanding-field-of-sensory-studies.

Howes, D. (2018). *Senses and Sensation: Critical and Primary Sources*. London: Bloomsbury Academic.

Huby, P. (2000). *Pasiphae*. Stockport: Dewi Lewis Publishing.

Humbert-Mougin, S. (2006). La 'crétomanie' dans les arts de la scène en France au temps de la revue *Le Voyage en Grèce*. In S. Basch and A. Farnoux, eds., *Le Voyage en Grèce 1934–1939. Du périodique de tourisme à la revue artistique. Actes du colloque international organisé à l'École française d'Athènes et à la Fondation Vassilis et Eliza Goulandris à Andros (23–26 Septembre 2004)*. Athens: École française d'Athènes, pp. 205–18.

Ingold, T. (2007). Materials against Materiality. *Archaeological Dialogues*, 14 (1), 1–16.

Jolas, B. and Menesse, A. (2013). Sur Schliemann: quelques remarques sur la voix, la musique et le livret. *Nouvelle revue d'esthétique*, 12(2), 173–84.

Jones, R. (1991). *Prince of the Lilies*. Victoria, Australia: McPhee Gribble.

Jung, R. (2016). "Friede den Hütten, Krieg den Palästen!" – In the Bronze Age Aegean. In H. Meller, H. P. Hahn, R. Jung, R. Risch, eds., *Arm und Reich – Zur Ressourcenverteilung in prähistorischen Gesellschaften. 8. Mitteldeutscher Archäologentag vom 22. bis 24. Oktober 2015 in Halle (Saale) / Rich and Poor – Competing for Resources in Prehistoric Societies. 8th Archaeological Conference of Central Germany, October 22–24, 2015 in Halle (Saale)*. Tagungen des Landesmuseums für Vorgeschichte Halle 14. Halle: Landesamt für Denkmalpflege und Archäologie Sachsen-Anhalt, Landesmuseum für Vorgeschichte, pp. 553–76.

Junyer, J. (1947). *Dance Index 6 (7)*. (https://archive.org/details/danceindexu nse_27)

Kardamitsi-Adami, M. (2009). *Ανάκτορα στην Ελλάδα*. Athens: Melissa.

Kazantzakis, N. (1938). *Οδύσεια*. Athens: Pyrsos.

Kazantzakis, N. (1958). *The Odyssey: A Modern Sequel*, trans. by F. Kimon. London: Secker and Warburg.

Kazantzakis, N. (1988). *At The Palace of Knossos*, trans. by T. and T. Vasils. London: Peter Owen.

Klee, P. (1920). Paul Klee. In K. Edschmid, ed., *Tribüne der Kunst und Zeit: Eine Schriftensammlung XIII. Schöpferische Konfession*, Berlin: Erich Reiss, pp. 28–40. https://commons.wikimedia.org/wiki/File:Schoepferische_ Konfession_-_Paul_Klee.pdf.

Korres, G. S. (1984). Neues zum Mausoleum Heinrich Schliemanns in Athen. *Boreas. Münstersche Beiträge zur Archäologie*, 7, 317–25.

Korres, G. S. and Korres, M. (1981). Das Mausoleum Heinrich Schliemanns auf dem Zantral-friedhof von Athen. *Boreas. Münstersche Beiträge zur Archäologie*, 4, 133–73.

Lacarrière, J. (1975). *L'été Grec : une Grèce quotidienne de 4000 ans*. Paris: Plon.

Lancaster, O. (1947). *Classical Landscape with Figures*. London: Murray.

Lapatin, K. (2002). *Mysteries of the Snake Goddess: Art, Desire, and the Forging of History*. Boston: Houghton Mifflin.

La Rosa, V. and Militello, P. (2006). Minoan Crete in 20th-century Italian Culture. In Y. Hamilakis and N. Momigliano, eds., *Archaeology and European Modernity: Producing and Consuming the 'Minoans'*. Padova: Bottega d'Erasmo (Ausilio), pp. 241–58.

Latour, B. (2005). *Reassembling the Social: An Introduction to Actor-Network Theory*. Oxford: Oxford University Press.

Lawrence, D. H. (2002). *The Complete Poems of D.H. Lawrence*. Ware: Wordsworth.

Lazarus, E. (1877). Agamemnon's Tomb, *Scribner's Monthly*, vol. XIV, no. 1, May 1877, 47 (https://archive.org/details/scribnersmonthly04newy).

MacGillivray, J. A. (2000). *Minotaur: Sir Arthur Evans and the Archaeology of the Minoan Myth*. London: Jonathan Cape.

Macintosh, F. (1997). Tragedy in Performance: Nineteenth- and Twentieth-century Productions. In P.E. Easterling, ed., *The Cambridge Companion to Greek Theatre*. Cambridge: Cambridge University Press, pp. 284–323.

Marabini Moevs, M. T. (1985). Gabriele D'Annunzio fra Winckelmann e Schliemann. In E. Paratore, ed., *D'Annunzio e la cultura germanica. Atti del VI convegno internazionale di studi dannunziani, Pescara, 3-5 maggio 1984*. Pescara: Centro Nazionale di Studi Dannunziani, pp. 63–74.

Marinatos, S. (1939). The Volcanic Destruction of Minoan Crete. *Antiquity*, 13(52), 425–39.

Marlowe, C. (2019). *Doctor Faustus*, edited by Paul Menzer. London: Methuen Drama.

Mauclair, C. (1934). *Le pur visage de la Grèce*. Paris: Grasset.

McDonald, W. A. and Thomas, C. G. (1990). *Progress into the Past: The Rediscovery of Mycenaean Civilization*, 2nd edition. Bloomington, IN: Indiana University Press.

Merezhkovsky, D. (1926 [1925]). *The Birth of the Gods: Tutankhamon in Crete*, trans. by N.A. Duddington. London: Dent & Sons.

Miller, D. (2005). *Materiality (Politics, History, and Culture)*. Durham, NC: Duke University Press.

Miller, H. (1941). *The Colossus of Maroussi*. New York: New Directions.

Momigliano, N. (2017a). Introduction. In N. Momigliano and A. Farnoux, eds., *Cretomania: Modern Desires for the Minoan Past*. London: Routledge, pp. 1–16.

Momigliano, N. (2017b). From Russia with Love: Minoan Crete and the Russian Silver Age. In N. Momigliano and A. Farnoux, eds., *Cretomania: Modern Desires for the Minoan Past*. London: Routledge, pp. 84–110.

Momigliano, N. (2020). *In Search of the Labyrinth: The Cultural Legacy of Minoan Crete*. London: Bloomsbury Academic.

Momigliano, N. (2021). Minoan Fakes and Fictions. In K. Lennart and J. Martínez, eds., *Tenue Est Mendacium: Rethinking Fakes and Authorship in Classical, Late Antique, & Early Christian Works*. Eelde: Barkhuis, pp. 293–314.

Momigliano, N. and Farnoux, A. (2017). *Cretomania: Modern Desires for the Minoan Past*. London: Routledge.

Moore, D. J., Rowlands, E., and Karadimas, N. (2014). *In search of Agamemnon: Early Travellers to Mycenae*. Cambridge: Cambridge Scholars Publishing.

Morris, C. (2006). From Ideologies of Motherhood to 'Collecting Mother Goddesses'. In Y. Hamilakis and N. Momigliano, eds., *Archaeology and European Modernity: Producing and Consuming the 'Minoans'*. Padova: Bottega d'Erasmo (Ausilio), pp. 69–78.

Morris, C. (2017). Lord of the Dance: Ted Shawn's Gnossienne and its Minoan Context. In N. Momigliano and A. Farnoux, eds., *Cretomania: Modern Desires for the Minoan Past*. London : Routledge, pp. 111–123.

Mosso, A. (1907). *The Palaces of Crete and their Builders*. London: Fisher Unwin.

Nisbet, G. (2006). *Ancient Greece in Film and Popular Culture*. Bristol: Bristol Phoenix.

Novelli, G. (1966). *Viaggio in Grecia*. Rome: Arco d'Alibert.

Novelli, G. (2019). *Scritti '43–'68*, edited by P. Bonani. Rome: Nero.

Palaima, T. G. and McDonough, C. M. (2016). Two Linear B Traveling Inscriptions from the University of the South in Sewanee, Tennessee and the Impact of the Decipherment of Linear B on the Scholarly and Public Imagination. In J. Driessen, ed., *Ra-pi-ne-u: Studies on the Mycenaean World Offered to Robert Laffineur for his 70th Birthday*. Louvain-la-Neuve: Presses Universitaires de Louvain, pp. 233–44.

Pappalardo, U. (2021). Das 'Ilíou Mélathron': Heinrich Schliemann Haus in Athen. *Antike Welt: Zeitschrift für Archäologie und Kulturgeschichte*, 1.2021, 55–63.

Perrot, G. and C. Chipiez (1894). *Histoire de l'Art dans l'Antiquité: Tome VI, La Grèce Primitive, l'Art Mycénien*. Paris: Hachette.

Petersen, D. (2015). Live from Troy: Embedded in the Trojan War. In M. M. Winkler, ed., *Return to Troy: New Essays on the Hollywood Epic*. Leiden: Brill, pp. 27–48.

Petrie, F. W. M. (1890). The Egyptian Bases of Greek History. *The Journal of Hellenic Studies*, 11, 271–77.

Pinacoteca di Brera (2001). *Un Milanese che parlava toscano: Lamberto Vitali e la sua collezione*. Milano: Electa.

Piperno, M., Zampieri, C. and Van Den Bossche, B. (in the press). *The Tales of Archaeology. Towards a Literary 'Memory Map' of the Mediterranean Space*. Leuven: Peeters.

Porter, D. (1996). *Crete*. Melbourne: Hyland House.

Preston, J. (2007). *The Dig*. London: Viking.

Quasimodo, S. (1958). *La Terra Impareggiabile*. Milan: Mondadori.

Quasimodo, S. (1983). *Complete Poems*, trans. by J. Bevan. London: Anvil Press Poetry.

Randi, E. (2009). 'La città morta': tra Sarah Bernhardt ed Eleonora Duse. In M. I. Biggi and P. Puppa, eds., *Voci e anime, corpi e scritture*. Roma: Bulzoni, pp. 243–52.

Renault, M. (1958). *The King Must Die*. London: Longman, Green and Co.

Renault, M. (1962). *The Bull from the Sea*. London: Longman, Green and Co.

Renault, M. (1969). Notes on the King Must Die. In T. McCormack, ed., *Afterwords: Novelists on their Novels*. New York: Harper and Row, pp. 81–7.

Renfrew, C. (1991). *The Cycladic Spirit: Masterpieces from the Nicholas P. Goulandris Collection*. London: Thames & Hudson.

Renfrew, C. (2003). *Figuring it out: What are we? Where do we come from? The parallel visions of artists and archaeologists*. London: Thames & Hudson.

Renfrew, C., Gosden, C., and DeMarrais, E. (2004). *Substance, Memory, Display: Archaeology and Art.* Cambridge: McDonald Institute for Archaeological Research.

Riggs, C. (2017). *Egypt: Lost Civilizations.* London: Reaktion Books.

Roessel, D. (2006). Happy Little Extroverts and Bloodthirsty Tyrants: Minoans and Mycenaeans in Literature in English after Evans and Schliemann. In Y. Hamilakis and N. Momigliano, eds., *Archaeology and European Modernity: Producing and Consuming the 'Minoans'.* Padova: Bottega d'Erasmo (Ausilio), pp. 197–208.

Rollinger, C. (2020). *Classical Antiquity in Video Games: Playing with the Ancient World.* London: Bloomsbury Academic.

Rooney, S. (2021). *Beautiful World, Where Are You.* London: Faber & Faber.

Runnels, C. (2007). *The Archaeology of Heinrich Schliemann: An Annotated Bibliographic Handlist,* 2nd edition. Boston: Archaeological Institute of America.

Russell, I. and Cochrane, A. (2015a) *Art and Archaeology: Collaborations, Conversations, Criticisms.* New York: Springer.

Russell, I. and Cochrane, A. (2015b). Introduction. In I. Russell, I. and A. Cochrane, eds., *Art and Archaeology: Collaborations, Conversations, Criticisms.* New York: Springer, pp. 1–8.

Saint, J. (2021). *Ariadne.* London: Wildfire.

Sallaska, G. (1971). *The Last Heracles.* New York: Doubleday.

Sallaska, G. (1974 [1971]). *The Last Heracles.* London: New English Library.

Sakellarakis, Y. and Sapouna-Sakellaraki, E. (1981). Drama of Death in a Minoan Temple. *National Geographic,* 159(2), 204–23.

Sakellarakis, Y. and Sakellarakis, E. (1997). *Archanes: Minoan Crete in a New Light.* Athens: Ammos.

Schliemann, H. (1875). *Troy and its Remains: a Narrative of Researches and Discoveries Made on the Site of Ilium, and in the Trojan Plain.* London: Murray.

Scott, G. (2016). *The Age of Treachery.* London: Titan Books.

Scott, G. (2017). *The Age of Olympus.* London: Titan Books.

Scott, G. (2018). *The Age of Exodus.* London: Titan Books.

Seferis, G. (2018). *Complete Poems,* trans. by E. Keeley and P. Sherrard. Manchester: Carcanet.

Shalev, Z. (2010). *Thera.* New Milford, CT: The Toby Press.

Shapland, A. (2013). Jumping to Conclusions? Bull-leaping in Minoan Crete. *Society and Animals,* 21, 194–207.

Shapland, A. (2021). Nicoletta Momigliano, *In Search of the Labyrinth: The Cultural Legacy of Minoan Crete. International Journal of the Classical Tradition*, 29, 231–3.

Shapland, A. (2022). *Human-Animal Relations in Bronze Age Crete. A History through Objects*. Cambridge: Cambridge University Press.

Shapland, A. (2023). *Labyrinth: Knossos, Myth & Reality*. Oxford: Ashmolean Museum.

Sideris, G. (1976), *Το Αρχαίο Θέατρο στη Νέα Ελληνική Σκηνή 1817–1932*. Athens: Ikaros.

Sitwell, S. (1933). *Canons of Giant Art: Twenty Torsos in Heroic Landscapes*. London: Faber & Faber.

Spengler, O. (1918). *Der Untergang des Abendlandes*: *Umrisse Einer Morphologie der Weltgeschichte*. Vienna: Braumüller.

Spengler, O. (1922). *Der Untergang des Abendlandes: Welthistorische Perspektiven*. Vienna: Braumüller.

Spengler, O. (1928). *The Decline of the West, v. 2: Perspectives of World-history*, trans. by C.F. Atkinson. New York: Knopf.

Swann, B. T. (1966). *Day of the Minotaur*. New York: Ace Books.

Swann, B. T. (1971). *The Forest Forever*. New York: Ace Books.

Swann, B. T. (1977). *Cry Silver Bells*. New York: Daw Books.

Sweetman, D. (1993). *Mary Renault: A Biography*. London: Chatto & Windus.

Thimme, J. (1977). *Art and Culture of the Cyclades in Third Millennium B.C.* Chicago: University of Chicago Press.

Traill, D. A. (1995). *Schliemann of Troy: Treasure and Deceit*. New York: St. Martin's Press.

Traill, D. A. (2014). Heinrich Schliemann, 1822–90, and Sophia Schliemann, 1852–1932: Searching for Homer's World. In B. Fagan, ed., *The Great Archaeologists*. London: Thames and Hudson, pp. 2–77.

Trigger, B. G. (2006). *A History of Archaeological Thought*, 2nd edition. Cambridge: Cambridge University Press.

Vermeule, E. T. (1964). *Greece in the Bronze Age*, Chicago: University of Chicago Press.

Wall, S., Musgrave, J., and Warren, P. (1986). Human Bones from a Late Minoan IB House at Knossos, *Annual of the British School at Athens*, 81, 333–88.

Wallace, J. (2004) *Digging the Dirt: The Archaeological Imagination*. London: Duckworth.

Warren, P. (1981a). Knossos: Stratigraphical Museum Excavations, 1978–1980. Part I. *Archaeological Reports*, 27, 73–92.

Warren, P. (1981b). Minoan Crete and Ecstatic Religion. Preliminary Observations on the 1979 Excavations at Knossos and Postscript on the

1980 Excavations at Knossos. In R. Hägg and N. Marinatos, eds., *Sanctuaries and Cults in the Aegean Bronze Age. Proceedings of the First International Symposium at the Swedish Institute in Athens, 12–13 May 1980.* Stockholm: Svenska Institutet i Athen, pp. 155–166.

Wells, H. G. (1920). *The Outline of History, Being a Plain History of Life and Mankind.* New York: Macmillan.

Wilde, O. (2003). *The Complete Works of Oscar Wilde Introduced by Merlin Holland,* 5th edition. London: HarperCollins.

Winkler, M. M. (2007). The Trojan War on the Screen: An Annotated Filmography. In M.M. Winkler, ed., *Troy: From Homer's Iliad to Hollywood Epic.* Malden, MA: Blackwell, pp. 201–15.

Winkler, M. M. (2015). Wolfgang Petersen on Homer and Troy. In M. M. Winkler, ed., *Return to Troy: New Essays on the Hollywood Epic.* Leiden : Brill, pp. 16–26.

Worth, N. (1924). *The Arms of Phaedra: A Tale of Wonder and Adventure.* London: Mills & Boon.

Yehoshua, A. B. (1992). *Mr Mani,* transl. by H. Halkin. San Diego, CA: Harcourt, Brace.

Zervos, C. (1934). *L'art en Grèce des temps préhistoriques au début du XVIIIe siècle.* Paris: Cahiers d'Art.

Zervos, C. (1957). *L'Art des Cyclades du début à la fin de l'Âge du bronze, 2500–1100 avant notre ère.* Paris: Cahiers d'Art.

Zilboorg, C. (2001). *The Mask of Mary Renault: A Literary Biography.* Columbia : University of Missouri Press.

Acknowledgments

I thank the editors of this Cambridge Series on the Aegean Bronze Age for inviting me to contribute with this Aegeomanic essay and the two anonymous reviewers for their kind comments and useful suggestions. I am also very grateful to Fritz Blakolmer, Oliver Dickinson, Tom Palaima, and Yannis Galanakis for sharing with me their knowledge of things Mycenaean, to Giacomo Loi for information on Israeli novels, and to Jan Driessen for showing me a draft of his forthcoming volume on the casts of the Lion Gate of Mycenae and perceptive comments on my Aegeomania. I thank David Constantine for fruitful and illuminating discussions of his poem 'Cycladic Idols' and other poems in his collection *The Pelt of Wasps*. The colleagues who helped me over the years with my interest in Cretomania are too numerous to be mentioned here (but see Momigliano 2020: xiii–xv, for starters). Many thanks are due to Geraldine Sommier, Directrice du Patrimoine at Chloè, for helping me with the illustrations of Karl Lagerfeld's creations inspired by the Thera frescoes. I am also indebted to the numerous artists and archivists who provided me with materials and permissions for my illustrations. The late Sally Humphreys read an early draft of this essay. With her customary frankness, she told me that she found the topic very boring, but was surprised by the amount of materials that I had found, and kindly improved my English. None of the above, however, should be responsible for any remaining faults. Readers should be aware that, although I have included new ideas and new materials (especially in Sections 1, 2, 4.6, 5.4, and 7), inevitably I also drew from my recent publication *In Search of the Labyrinth: The Cultural Legacy of Minoan Crete* (2020), where I cover some elements discussed in this essay in greater detail and provide more contextualisation in terms of historical and disciplinary developments. I also drew on a very short essay submitted to editors in 2016, but still unpublished at the time of writing this essay (2023/24), which is mentioned in note 1. My gratitude to my late husband, Roger H. Lonsdale, remains undiminished, even if he is no longer with us.

Cambridge Elements

The Aegean Bronze Age

Carl Knappett

University of Toronto

Carl Knappett is the Walter Graham/ Homer Thompson Chair in Aegean Prehistory
at the University of Toronto.

Irene Nikolakopoulou

Hellenic Ministry of Culture, Archaeological Museum of Heraklion

Irene Nikolakopoulou is an archaeologist and curator at the Archaeological Museum
of Heraklion, Crete.

About the Series

This series is devised thematically to foreground the conceptual developments
in the Aegean Bronze Age, one of the richest subfields of archaeology, while reflecting
the range of institutional settings in which research in this field is conducted.
It aims to produce an innovative and comprehensive review of the latest scholarship in
Aegean prehistory.

Cambridge Elements ≡

The Aegean Bronze Age

Elements in the Series

Printed in the United States
by Baker & Taylor Publisher Services